Land the Perfect Job
In an Imperfect Market

Strategies to help break through the job search clutter

By Joseph Ortenzi, MA, CRC

The Professionals Say

Concise! This book flows well from page to page with the "Best of the Best" of job search strategies in the market. It is creatively written with real life examples for a successful job search. Each chapter will be an asset to anyone entering the job market. Great work!

Jerry Grimes, M.A., CRC, VA Counseling Psychologist

I have been exposed to many books that provide information on how to find a job, but most are highly technical and are not geared to the average job seeker. Mr. Ortenzi's book is a great tool for those individuals who need a hand up, not just a handout. He has managed to put together a simple but dynamic tool that anyone seeking employment can use. His down to earth illustrations relate to that average person and foster hope for the reader. If you want assistance in securing employment in a very practical way, this book is your answer.

Benjamin W. Butler, M.A., Former Department of Veterans Affairs Vocational Rehabilitation and Employment Officer for the state of Pennsylvania

"In my 30+ years as a Vocational Rehabilitation Counselor and manager of a vocational rehabilitation program, I have long maintained that job seeking is truly an art form. In order for the desired goal to be achieved, the process must be fluid, adaptive, and ever-changing in response to new information and outcomes attained in each step of the journey. "Land the Perfect Job in an Imperfect Market" eliminates the mystique associated with job-seeking in an entertaining, enlightening, and thought-provoking manner!

Mr. Ortenzi presents out of the box and easy-to-understand perspectives with which to view the job search process, and broaden the conceptual framework of the reader. The book then offers step by step; practical can do instructions, with samples that the reader can incorporate into their job search style.

MOST IMPORTANT, "Land the Perfect Job in an Imperfect Market" is about EMPOWERMENT of the job seeker and the personal value one can attain by taking full control of their job search. The wisdom imparted in this guide will be a great asset to the job seeker.

It is my most profound pleasure to have worked and laughed with Mr. Ortenzi in serving disabled workers throughout my career. It is an honor as well to lend my full endorsement to "Land the Perfect Job in an Imperfect Market."

John R. Arnett M.Ed.
Vocational Rehabilitation Counselor

"Land the Perfect Job in an Imperfect Market" is entertaining, enriching and enlightening. This is a remarkable book. Mr. Ortenzi shares a wealth of experiences for anyone seeking employment. Excellent source of information for a successful job search.

Kathy Trumm, CDMS, CCM

What his clients say:

"I consider the chance to write this endorsement for the book written by Mr. Joe Ortenzi an honor. A perfect title "Land the Perfect Job in an Imperfect Market" is, in my opinion, spectacular.

I met Joe when I was unable to work, and I continue to stay in touch with him because of his wit, charm, enthusiasm and knowledge. Joe encourages you to think outside of the box to utilize your unique style when searching for employment.

This book is written in such a brilliant way just like the way he talks with you personally. When you are looking for employment no matter the reason just reading this book will give you the great ideas combined with enthusiasm and real-world experience. It is, in fact, a step by step guide showcased with examples of real life experience.

I continue to utilize the words of wisdom and a feeling of empowerment from Joe Ortenzi and have shared these with many in their search for employment and will be encouraging them to buy this book. I encourage all to read and purchase this book." - Shelma Bockey

- **Shelma:** "I hear from people that give feedback that my resume looks impressive, and my credentials are amazing and easy to find. My resume looks uncluttered and easy to read. My key points stand out."

- **Donna:** "I just got a call from (employer) about an interview. It is set for April 8th, but I just had to tell you what the girl said. She said that she thought that my resume was one of the best she had ever seen. Straight forward and to the point and all on one page. She was going to design her kids resume from your format. By the way, I didn't tell her that I didn't do it."

- **Laura:** "Employers are swamped with paperwork. The person that is conducting an interview said it is wonderful to have such colorful information on the resume. They have commented on this new approach to a resume. The clarity gives them something to talk about immediately. Employers want to know if you are qualified for the position right in their office. The resume you created gave real information and it was not generic. The references are listed with live comments."

ALL RIGHTS RESERVED.

©2016 by **Joseph A. Ortenzi**. Except as provided by the Copyright Act December 4, 2014, no part of this publication may be reproduced, stored in a retrieval system or transmitted in any form or by any means without the prior written permission of the publisher."

Preface and Acknowledgments

This book is about you. But before I begin, allow me to introduce myself. For the last 16 years, I have operated Skills Enrichment Group. My company focused on return-to-work services. I provide transitional employment services, vocational evaluations, vocational feasibility evaluations, transferable skills analyzes, vocational explorations, employment workshops and vocational consulting.

Before starting my company, I was a Senior Counseling Psychologist managing vocational rehabilitation services for veterans with disabilities at the Department of Veterans Affairs.

My on-going practice provides assistance to clients non-disabled and disabled. This book addresses the barriers to employment that all job seekers encounter. Because of the major barriers many of my clients faces, I have developed a different approach to finding suitable employment.

Three chapters are contributions from professional associates with expertise in their fields:

Chapter 2 - Marketing 101 - Finding a Job... Selling Beer — Kinda, the Same, was written by Jim Tabaczynski. He has more than 40 years communications experience including agency and corporate public relations. He holds an M.A. in Journalism/Public Relations and is a member of the Counselors Academy of the Public Relations Society of America.

Chapter 3 - Help the Long Suffering Recruiter, was written by Doug Nolan, an independent recruiter for over 19 years. He started Key Search in 1996 after five years as a financial analyst in private industry. He has provided qualified candidates for dozens of major and medium size corporations. Doug has an MBA in Finance and a Bachelor's degree in economics from Cleveland State University. He currently serves on the Alumni Board at CSU's College of Business.

Chapter 15 -The Sales Interview – Selling a Most Important Product, was written by Ron Finklestein. He is called the "Real Deal" by his clients. He is the creator of the Business Growth Experience and owner of RPF Group Inc. Ron is a consultant, international author, sales trainer and speaker. His six business books cover management and leadership, personaldevelopment, operations, marketing, and sales. His latest book: "Make a Difference: From Success to Significance" was a 12-year study of 1,000 successful small business owners and what they did to be successful.

Note: The resume and cover letter samples provided in the book are written mostly by my clients with my coaching. They do not meet all the perfect standards outlined in many articles about cover letters and resumes. These have worked for the employed clients. They were creative, and the clients owned the results.

I suffered greatly at the hands of my two editors, Ben Bonnano and Jim Tabaczynski. If the text is not perfect, blame them.

Land the Perfect Job in an Imperfect Market

Table of Contents

Introduction		VII
1.	Designing, Yes, Designing a Resume	1
2.	Marketing 101 - Finding a Job… Selling Beer — Kind of the Same	5
3.	Help the Long Suffering Recruiter	13
4.	The Dreaded Screening Software	21
5.	"Any Road Will Take You There"	25
6.	No One is "The Perfect Candidate."	31
7.	Your Story is Unique. Stand Out From the Crowd	37
8.	Everything You've Read About Resumes is True (Sort Of)	41
9.	Power of Testimonials	44
10.	Your "Draft" Resume – a Work in Progress	49
11.	Where Has the Day Gone?	65
12.	Networking, Information Interview, Warm Contacts	67
13.	Maximizing the Power of LinkedIn and Other On-line Employment Sites	73
14.	Now What? I Have the Tools. How? Where? Why?	75
15.	The Sales Interview – Selling the Most Important Product	77
16.	Creative Follow-Ups, Creating a Magic List	91
17.	Survive and Thrive in a Dynamic Job Market, Ideas for Life	95

Land the Perfect Job in an Imperfect Market

Introduction

While employed by the Department of Veterans Affairs, I said in a white paper:

> We believe that the next ten years will be a continuation of job markets that include temporary, part-time, downsizing, core employees, contracted services, specialized skills, reduced benefits, and self-employment. Veterans not only need to have skills and knowledge needed in these job markets, but the ability to survive and thrive in these job markets.

What has changed? Nothing. In fact, what was predicted then is even truer today, with multiple recessions over the last 20 years, exporting jobs, supply and demand of workers, major innovations in technology, and computerization. These factors are beyond any institution to impact. There is a real possibility that there will be a large group of people who will not find gainful employment in their lifetimes.

This brings us to our current concern: How can YOU find suitable employment in a chaotic job market with many applicants chasing limited job openings? What skills and knowledge do employers and applicants need to make a job match? How can you find the decision-makers amid the job-screening, impersonal software and contract recruiters? What kind of employment barriers do you have? How will you make the first cut?

You need a new mindset! In the current job market, you need to consider yourself self-employed. There are no long-term social contracts for employment, if they ever existed.

You bring skills, experience, and work habits to the employer. The employer has a problem to solve. As long as there is a balance between your needs and the needs of the employer, you will have stable employment.

You have a responsibility to yourself to continue to build skills and determine what additional skills are in demand with your employer and the job market. You are on a continual learning curve for the rest of your working career if you are to thrive. We will discuss what you can do in Chapter 8.

Is your head spinning yet? Is there a rational approach to finding employment? Yes, but it is a project with many elements to address. The best qualified do not always get the job. Finding a job is an accident; a perfect storm, so to speak. What you need is to produce quality accidents by marketing yourself carefully, being creative, going where others do not, working your networks, organizing your time, being persistent and out-hustling other applicants.

Finding a job might appear to be an overwhelming task. If you have been searching with no results, you may feel discouraged and out of control; that might affect your self-esteem. We all need to feel we have some control over our careers and our lives.

The best approach is to recognize that there are many factors that we cannot control. We can take charge of a job search with an active, focused strategy that produces "quality accidents;" at the right place, right time with the right presentation.

Before beginning your job search, a little self-examination is required: Are you clearly focused on the type of job and type of company you want and the job you're willing to accept? Have you considered that you have barriers to overcome to find the right job? How will you address these in a resume, cover letter, and interview?

What kind of an employee are you? All the elements of the job search are indicators as to who you are, and how you will operate in the workplace. So, the messages you give out with phone calls, cover letters, resumes, emails, on-line social networks, professional networks, physical appearance, organization, interviews and follow-ups are examples to employers of your future performance. Each of these areas provides you an opportunity to excel.

Are you ready to begin? Sorry, a free on-line resume produced by a software program will not help you stand out from the crowd. You need to tell your story so that the real you comes through.

The focus of this book is to develop a customized basic resume that can be modified as necessary. The book will also help you develop a basic cover letter to tell your story and help you stand out from the crowd.

Also, we will provide job search strategies for using your new tools in an effective manner.

The human resource specialist dilemma: Early in my career, I read a book on how to find employment written by a human resources specialist. The basic theme was to do everything that Human Resources ask you to do. Later when I was the human resources specialist, I understood the logic of that approach.

I was recruiting for a clothing warehouse with seasonal staffing needs that varied wildly from quarter to quarter.

Because I was getting a large number of applicants for each job opening, my approach was to gather as much information as possible with limited applicant contact. I remember spreading out resumes on a large table searching for reasons to eliminate applicants. The bigger companies today use applicant tracking systems/automated resume screeners to reduce the number of applicants they will contact. Unavoidably, *many good candidates are screened out before being given any consideration*. All this achieves is securing employment for the HR specialist.

Why do you not get calls: The first and sometimes second screening, is to determine who does not meet the company's requirements. Hopefully, this book will assist you to survive the first and second screening so you can meet with a real person and impress them with your story. Better, it will help you find ways to contact decision-makers that do not include the Internet ads. A sure-fire resume and cover letter are not enough. If you are looking for a quick fix, do not waste your time on this or any other book. As you might have heard, looking for a job is a job in itself.

I promise you lots of homework. The good news is you will have an approach to long-term careers. Note the word "careers." Your employment may involve many jobs and several careers.

We will assist you with information, ideas, techniques and inspiration to be creative. Hopefully, you will go where others have not gone. We will provide many samples to allow you a feel of what others have done and been successful.

You have a step up on the competition: If you read eBooks, you probably have access to the Internet, a computer, a tablet and a smartphone. Hopefully, you have a working knowledge of word processing. If not, find help for your word processing skills. Your job search and most jobs require basic skills. Many of my clients have no computer skills. In the current job market, this is a major barrier.

Last, many books and articles on the Internet focus on the needs of college educated, upper-level management and professional job seekers. Most jobs do not require a four year college education. This book is a guide for all levels of the job search that include manufacturing workers, office support, technicians, transportation workers, tradesman, managers, professionals, veterans and recent graduates.

Chapter 1 - Designing. Yes, Designing a Resume

In my early 20's, I sold my aquarium and beautiful fish to purchase a single lens reflex camera. My new hobby would be to create beautiful pictures. As I looked thru the lens, I saw things I had never seen before. There were shades of light, shapes created by shadows, textures, perspectives near and far, perfectly balanced landscapes and portraits - all of which made a statement.

What I saw was always there. The lens caused me to raise my awareness of my surroundings. Within each of us is a creative understanding of what pleases the eye, of balance, of comfort and effective communication.

Look through your lens at resumes. Artists view other's art; writers read other's works. Effective job seekers look at examples others have done, not just to copy the examples, but to incorporate principles, ideas and approaches for a new creative product.

The Basics of Formatting a Resume or Cover Letter

Here's a conundrum: You want your resume and cover letter to stand out from the crowd, but still, there are some basic rules and guidelines that you should follow. And, no, this is not an oxymoron. Rather, when creating an effective resume and cover letter, we hold these truths to be self-evident:

Appearance: Hold your resume at arm's length. Is it pleasing to the eye? Is it balanced?

Short and sweet: Shorter sentences are more readable and easier to comprehend. Most sentences should not exceed 15-18 words in length (a limit of five ideas) - See: Strunk and White - *Elements of Style*. If you don't have a copy, most libraries do.

Notice me!! Be judicious in your use of bold text, italics, underlining, and bullets. Be conscious of centering and spacing.

Same can be good: To maximize the appearance and readability of your document, use the same type font throughout.

Wide open spaces: Don't be afraid to include white space. You don't want your document to appear busy or copy intensive. Do not overwhelm your reader with print.

Can you see me now? Choose interesting, but readable fonts. Do not use Arial or Times New Roman. Verdana is one of the several fonts that was developed especially to be more readable on computer monitors.

Sample Fonts (all in 12 point)

Georgia:	Am I pleasing to the eye and readable?
Garamond:	Am I pleasing to the eye and readable?
Trebuchet:	Am I pleasing to the eye and readable?
Verdana:	Am I pleasing to the eye and readable?

I suggest boxes to create a resume. They help position the elements to achieve balance. The following illustrates the use of boxes. After constructing the resume, you mark the boxes and make the borders invisible.

Note: Designing your resume assumes you have a good working knowledge of word processing. Some people do not have enough knowledge to setup spacing, boxes, and dividing lines. If you fall into this group, developing skills in word processing is essential. Check out free training at your local library. Or, go to my website and review the samples resumes at http://www.jobsearchstrategies.net/.

There are a number of "free resume" sites on the Internet that will help create a resume. Using the information in this book, modify the "free resume."

Tip: Saving your final version as a PDF - it will preserve the formatting if you are sending your resume as an email attachment to an employer.

In chapter 10 you will find some sample resumes. The clients are real with barriers to employment. Look at the formats and how the content is presented. In Chapter 7, you will read their stories and how their stories are used in cover letters and resumes. All have located employment using these marketing tools. They are a tow truck driver, administrative assistant, project manager, retail sales clerk and electronic technician.

The two resumes below show the boxes used to position the text and then the final text with the boxes gone.

Find some sample resumes on the Internet. Are they visually appealing? How quickly can you review qualifications? Are the sentences easy to read?

# Ike Smith	123 Grove Drive Cleveland, Ohio 44099 (440) 992-9999 Cell (440) 969-9999 ikesmith@yahoo.com

Summary of Qualifications

Experienced warehouse/shipping & receiving management; operate forklifts, cranes, bobcats, lifts; extensive maintenance, including HVAC; fabricating/design sheet metal, steel, includes welding

Profile

High energy, learn new skills quickly; pride in work, timely; reliable; realize the Importance of meeting deadlines as scheduled; self-motivated and capable of organizing a variety of activities.

Strengths and Skills

- Managed and supervised employees, trained staff, planned and scheduled work, inventory and warehouse management	- Remodeling including: hanging cabinets, countertops, trim, windows, doors, painting, dry walling, plumbing & pipefitting, electrical install	- All aspects of form, frame, finish carpentry, experienced with heating and air conditioning units
- Equipment operator forklifts 2,000 to 20,000 lbs, man lifts 20' to 120,' articulating, scissor, straight boom lifts, small cranes drivable, bobcats, operator of plant bridge & jib cranes up to 100 ton.	- Diversified in installation & servicing of material handling systems, material conveying systems. - Design & troubleshooting of Customized Ventilation and Air Filtration Systems. - Hydraulics (hi & low pressure)	- Fabrication & installation of sheet metal products and systems. - Steel fabrication & design, welding in gas, Arc, Mig, Tig. - Some electrical single phase and 3-phase.

Professional experience and position titles:

Lathe Cut Set-up Technician-1 & Lathe Cut Service and Supply-2, Installation Supervisor, Automotive Technician, Maintenance Technician, Injection Mold Setter / Maintenance

Education and Technical Skills

Cleveland High School/ACJVS Graduate, Ohio Diesel Automotive Technical School - Major studies automotive technician/advanced studies

Ike Smith

123 Grove Drive
Cleveland, Ohio 44099
(440) 992-9999
Cell (440) 969-9999
ikesmith@yahoo.com

Summary of Qualifications

Experienced warehouse/shipping & receiving management; operate forklifts, cranes, bobcats, lifts; extensive maintenance, including HVAC; fabricating/design sheet metal, steel, includes welding

Profile

High energy, learn new skills quickly; pride in work, timely; reliable; realize the Importance of meeting deadlines as scheduled; self-motivated and capable of organizing a variety of activities.

Strengths and Skills

- Managed and supervised employees, trained staff, planned and scheduled work, inventory and warehouse management
- Equipment operator forklifts 2,000 to 20,000 lbs, man lifts 20' to 120,' articulating, scissor, straight boom lifts, small cranes drivable, bobcats, operator of plant bridge & jib cranes up to 100 ton.
- Remodeling including: hanging cabinets, countertops, trim, windows, doors, painting, dry walling, plumbing & pipefitting, electrical install
- Diversified in installation & servicing of material handling systems, material conveying systems.
- Design & troubleshooting of Customized Ventilation and Air Filtration Systems.
- Hydraulics (hi & low pressure)
- All aspects of form, frame, finish carpentry, experienced with heating and air conditioning units
- Fabrication & installation of sheet metal products and systems.
- Steel fabrication & design, welding in gas, Arc, Mig, Tig.
- Some electrical single phase and 3-phase.

Professional experience and position titles:

Lathe Cut Set-up Technician-1 & Lathe Cut Service and Supply-2,
Installation Supervisor, Automotive Technician, Maintenance Technician,
Injection Mold Setter / Maintenance

Education and Technical Skills

Cleveland High School/ACJVS Graduate, Ohio Diesel Automotive
Technical School - Major studies automotive technician/advanced studies

Chapter 2 - Marketing 101

Finding a Job... Selling Beer — Kinda the Same

By Jim Tabaczynski.

There are those who believe (and I happen to agree with them) that a job search is essentially a marketing and sales process. In the marketing phase, you create your product - which happens to be yourself - dress it up, clean it up, make it look as good as it possibly can - and then sell it to a potential employer. That's it in a nutshell. When your selling process is successful, you've got yourself a job.

To realize the full benefit of the process you probably should have some idea of what constitutes a sound marketing approach. This may be more difficult than it first appears. Unfortunately, many people mistakenly use the terms marketing and sales interchangeably, but the two functions - although interrelated - are very different.

Ideally, most of your marketing efforts should be completed before you venture out to begin selling. Your marketing program may not end there, however. As you proceed through your selling efforts, you may find that you may need to modify your marketing plan. That's not unusual. It happens all the time.

In this chapter, we present an overview of the marketing function so that you can see how to apply it to your job search. In the real world of marketing, every plan is unique. While every plan may not contain every element to be discussed here, there are a lot of similarities and constants – and that is where we will focus our attention.

Where to Start?

Oscar Hammerstein wrote, "Let's start at the very beginning. A very good place to start."

So, what is our starting point? That would be our product. In this case, it's you! So what about you? What can you do? And, perhaps just as important, what can't you do? Where can you do it? Where have you done it? Where would you like to do it next?

These are all good questions, but to wrap your arms around the process, it would help to have some sort of framework. Fortunately, the marketing gurus have given you one. It's called a SWOT analysis. Used mainly for companies and products, you can perform a SWOT analysis on yourself as well.

By the way, SWOT stands for Strengths, Weaknesses, Opportunities, and Threats. Sounds a little bit like the questions we posed a couple of paragraphs back, doesn't it.

Strengths: What are your strengths? Maybe you have 20 years experience doing whatever it is that you do. Maybe you're adept at handling a variety of types of equipment. Maybe you've mastered several kinds of software. Maybe you shine at cutting costs or managing people. Any of those can be strengths. From these strengths – and it's more than OK to have more than one – you can create a summary of qualifications for yourself. This also will give you a good sense of where to look for your next position.

Weaknesses: Do we really need to cover this? Yeah, I'm afraid we do. Honestly, what are your weaknesses? (Honestly is the key word there. Actually "honestly" is the key word throughout this entire endeavor.) Maybe you haven't mastered that software. Maybe the only kind of equipment that you can run is the obsolete relics that your former employer was trying to squeeze a few more years out of. Maybe you have physical limitations that prevent you from performing certain tasks. Maybe you were never given an opportunity to be put into a leadership position.

Keep in mind, your weaknesses don't make you bad person. It simply means that these are not your strong points. No one excels at everything. No one!

Why do we need to do this? Knowing and accepting your shortcomings may help eliminate some positions and/or companies where, realistically, you don't have a snowball's chance of getting through the door. This can save you considerable time as well as the burden of rejection. Let's focus our efforts on the positive.

Opportunities: This is where we play match.com with your strengths. You're strong at X, Y and Z; here's a company that thrives on X, Y and Z. So which are those companies? Make a list. Eliminate the ones that may be geographically impractical for you to reach (i.e., commute.) Target the companies that are in an industry where you have experience.

Let's match your skills with their needs. Those are opportunities. How to find them? Scan the business news. Talk to your friends and colleagues. Who might be open to adding staff?

Threats: Then, there's the bad news. What can prevent you from locking in with one of these companies? Maybe there's a burnt bridge in your past. Maybe your most promising company was just bought out by a foreign competitor, and they'll be cutting people before hiring any. Maybe it's a youth-oriented company, and you're... well, not so young anymore. Threats can come from anywhere. The good news is that 98 percent of the time, they're not your fault. Get over it. Move on. As with your weaknesses, you don't want to waste time and effort on a not-so-promising target.

Key Messages

To successfully market a product, everyone on board needs to know about the product so that you can deliver a clear, distinct, consistent message. It could be that your product is new or re-designed, or cheaper, larger or smaller, more efficient, more cost effective, the first of its kind, a vast improvement over anything in the market today. What can I say about this product that might make someone want to purchase it?

In marketing yourself, you must decide what to emphasize and what to highlight as well as what to downplay (Maybe your strengths?). These messages may vary somewhat depending on the person you're contacting, the job in question, or the industry in which you're entering.

This brings us to a very important juncture. This point is absolutely critical for the product marketer and the job seeker alike, and it may be the most difficult part of the process. And that point is honesty. There's that word again.

It is incredibly difficult for some product managers to look at their products honestly and give a straight-from-the-hip appraisal of what their product can do (and can't do) and why it's worth whatever you hope to be charging for it.

The same is true for the job seeker. You may think you ran the department at your last job, but can you give yourself that title on your resume. Not a good idea. Can you detail what your functions were and what successes you had? Absolutely. But, again, you have to be painfully honest. If, because of you, sales went up 12 percent – great! But 12 percent is not "nearly 25 percent." Can you round up 12 percent? Maybe, but in no one's math does 12 = 25.

"But everyone lies on their resumes!" This is a tired, old argument, to be sure. One can also say that people murder each other every day too, but that doesn't make it right. On any number of fronts, you're better off not getting a job by being honest, than landing a job based on a lie (or an exaggeration, or an embellishment) and having to explain it when you're found out. (And, don't kid yourself, eventually you will be found out.)

Now back to the matters at hand.

Features, Advantages, and Benefits

Every successful product has these three elements. To help distinguish one from the other and to help appreciate the differences, we'll use the example of automobile tires.

Features. Features are those elements of the product that make it new, special, or worthy of the customer's interest. In automobile tires, it may be the composite of which the tire is made; or, it might be the tread design.

Advantages. Advantages have to do with why these features are important. A new composite of automobile tire may result in the tire wearing longer. A new tread design may provide better handling.

Benefits. The benefits are how the customer profits from these advantages. Having a tire that wears longer is a financial benefit. You're getting more tire for your money. The improved handling may make your vehicle easier to drive or to enhance safety.

	AUTOMOBILE TIRE	**JOB APPLICANT**
FEATURES	New composite materials. New tread design.	Examples: Education. Work history. Industry experience. Skills.
ADVANTAGES	Wears longer. Improved handling.	Examples: Needs less training. Able to hit the ground running. Can deal with new circumstances + challenges. Good fit for your company.
BENEFITS	Saves money. Makes the car safer.	Immediately productive + more productive. Better return on the employer's investment.

Audience

If you're marketing a product, you have to ask yourself: Who do I need to reach to be successful in my plan? It could be the end-use customer. It could be a key decision maker who doesn't actually use the product but is integral to making the purchasing decision. It could be a dealer or distributor. It could be a purchasing manager. It could be a retail outlet that would stock your product. It could include a government regulator. It all depends on your product(s) and the industry where you do business.

As a job seeker, your key audiences are also varied. They are human resource professionals, recruiters (or headhunters), the final decision makers – which could be the person making the hiring decision, or the person for whom you would be working (who are not necessarily the same person). Also, you need to include colleagues, friends, family, or former co-workers and vendors, etc.; anyone who can assist in your quest.

Work Your Plan

Finally, we reach the real meat and potatoes of your plan. Again, the similarities with products and job searches are intriguing to say the least.

Let's start with the overall goal. In business, the overall goal is almost invariably to make money. In the job search, it's simply to find – not just a job, but the job that you want; the job that provides for you financially and professionally. You want a job that you will find satisfying and fulfilling. With your goal in place, we turn our attention to the

objectives, strategies, and tactics. "Wait a minute. Shouldn't the objective be to get a job?" Well, you're close. Let's do some hypothetical comparisons.

	MARKETING PLAN	JOB SEARCH
OBJECTIVES	Get established in a new territory. Take market share from a competitor. Become the low-cost (or high-end) product in the market.	Develop a list of suitable target companies in my industry or geographic area. Secure no less than x-number of interviews in the first month of your job search.

STRATEGIES	Create a new distribution network. Re-tool the product; design new packaging. Commit to an aggressive advertising and/or social media campaign. Develop a list of target customers who are critical to your campaign.	Employ multiple sources of potential company factual information (i.e. library reference lists + lists compiled from contacts with former co-workers, vendors, etc.) Supplement factual information with subjective information regarding company plans, industry developments, etc. Use this information to learn what is important and/or trending at your target companies.
TACTICS	Utilize your new distributor network to get the word on the street about your new endeavor. Selectively target your advertising to reach new target customers and/or to coincide with a key industry trade show.	Leverage the information from your research to gain a foot in the door of your target companies (new markets, new products, new competencies – and how you're a good fit) to secure interviews. Follow up with all contacts (successful or not) to maintain relationships with them that can be useful down the road.

"Remember: your resume is a marketing brochure, not a blueprint that documents your career history." – business2community.com

Chapter 3 - Help the Long Suffering Recruiter

By Doug Nolan

Working with a Recruiter

When searching for a new opportunity, working with a recruiter is only one weapon that a candidate could or should utilize. However, there are some things to keep in mind should you choose to pursue working with a recruiter and to continue to conduct your own search.

First, let the recruiter know where you have submitted your resume over the past three months. If there is duplication, it makes all parties look bad and employers may back off a candidate to avoid a mess. I don't believe you have to disclose where you're at in the interview process, but it's important to let them know not to pursue that company.

Some candidates like to know where recruiters have submitted their resume. I've known many candidates who wanted me to disclose that before I submitted their resume. I'm somewhat mixed on this. I believe a recruiter owes it to a candidate to let them know where they've been presented, however.

It's worth noting that most opportunities are found not through recruiters, but through avenues such as personal networking, colleague referrals, direct contact and responding to ads.

I believe that the more information a candidate shares with a recruiter, the better able the recruiter can assist. Sounds obvious? But, investing some time to disclose in-depth details regarding your employment history, culture desired and especially any special circumstances, will empower them to go to bat for you and enable them to swing at the best pitches.

One advantage of utilizing a recruitment firm is that they may have inroads to certain employers and/or job openings that have not been made public. Employers may not disclose that they are looking to fill a certain position for a variety of reasons, such as:

- They may want to keep it from their competitors.
- They may be replacing someone within their own company.
- They don't want to advertise that they are losing people.

Through their contacts, recruiters may have knowledge of other openings within certain companies that are posted publicly. This is especially true for larger companies with operations in several states. For the candidate who is willing to relocate, this can be a tremendous advantage.

As a candidate, you do not owe it to the recruiter to not continue conducting your own job search. However, treat the recruiter with respect and keep in mind their service is free of charge to you. The employer pays recruiters and, if and only when they successfully match their candidate with an open position. As a recruiter, I assume that clients are following leads on their own. I would only ask to let me know where they have submitted resumes or applications so as to avoid duplication.

Or, if there is no interest on behalf of the employer – or the candidate, the resume is typically filed.

A colleague prepared this excellent summary of the typical recruiting process.

Step one: The contract relationship is between the recruiter and the employer, not between recruiter and candidate.

Step two: The recruiter collects resumes from candidates for their client's jobs by searching various databases by function, keyword search or networking.

Step three: The recruiter then contacts candidate(s) for initial screenings. During such screenings, the recruiter presents an overview of opportunity, seeking to confirm both parties mutual interest. If the candidate is interested, the recruiter gathers data on the candidate's experience and goals. The recruiter also reviews where else has the candidate been presented and gets salary information.

Only when the process gets to this point does the recruiter disclose the company name and/or location. The recruiter then gets permission from the candidate to present his or her resume to the client.

Step four: The recruiter gets feedback from client – the prospective employer. If the feedback from the employer is favorable, the recruiter will discuss the next steps with the candidate as well as the employer.

Before the interview

All recruiters are different in how they prepare candidates for interviews – live or electronic. Here are examples of how one recruiter prepared her candidates for an in-person interview and a phone interview.

A recruiter's email preparing an applicant for a face-to-face with the decision-maker

> In preparation for your meeting with (interviewer), (interviewer's title) on January 2nd, I thought I would send you a few tips for a successful interview:
>
> - Check out the location of where you are meeting, ensuring you are on time.
> - Arrive 5 minutes early.
> - Dress professionally.
> - Take a few copies of your resume with you. (It's always nice to offer one to anyone you meet at an interview.)
> - If you have a two-fold, leather-like portfolio, that is a good thing to use for your resumes.
> - Also, have pen and paper with the portfolio.
> - Be sure to take extra time to review our website. This job will focus on our products.
> - Have questions about the job, the customers, training, career path, etc.
> - Ask for the interviewer's business card so you can follow-up with a thank-you email after the interview.
> - **Think about what you can do for the organization** – not just what we can do for you.
> - Pump up your energy and make good eye contact so they know you want the job.
> - Think about customer service that is a key part of this job!
>
> Let me know if you have any questions.
>
> We appreciate your interest in our company!
>
>
> Kind Regards,
>
> Susan

A recruiter's email preparing an applicant for a phone interview with decision-maker

Hello, Doug!

I am excited to hear that (interviewer's name), (interviewer's title) has contacted you and has set up an appointment on Monday for a phone interview.

One of the biggest things to communicate during the interview is your customer service skills, which will come across in your voice and energy on the phone. For example, (interviewer's name) might want to know how you develop a rapport with people, how well you work on a team, what you have done to go above and beyond the call of duty on a job, and how you handle unhappy customers while keeping the company policies in mind, etc.

Interpersonal communication skills and customer service, are the most important parts of the (title's) job! We can train someone how to service our equipment, but the customer service part of this job is something that the successful candidate brings with them to the job.

Think about what you can do for our organization – not just what we can do for you. Be sure to pump up your energy so (interviewer's name) knows you want the job and why it excites you! Make sure, if you haven't already, to watch the video and review our website again, so you are knowledgeable about what we do. Thank (interviewer's name) for taking the time to talk to you, and be sure to follow up with a thank-you email. His email address is (name)@gmail.com.

Please let me know if you have any questions and GOOD LUCK!

Kind Regards,

Susanne

Susanne, the Midwest corporate recruiter

My colleague, Jim Tabaczynski and I had several discussions with Susanne about her experiences. She was reviewing her previous week's contacts and the carefulpreparation she provided for a candidate referred to a manager.

For his newsletter, Nifty50s Jim wrote the following:

Is this too much to ask?

10 Reasons Why Companies Can't Fill Positions

We hear a lot about job seekers enduring protracted job searches while we also hear that companies have jobs that they can't fill. Sounds like some sort of disconnect. Here is another in our ongoing Nifty Series of Views from the Other Side of the Desk.

This list is courtesy of a recruiter from a $2 billion Midwest corporation with 10,000 employees. She says, "We can't find enough people to fill our positions that…"

1. Come with the right attitude to the phone interview and can speak in complete sentences.
2. Are willing to take the time to prepare for the interview.
3. Have a decent and professional resume – at least without typos, misspelled words and incorrect dates or information.
4. Have done five minutes of research on my company.
5. Have not had a DUI in five years… I would like to say **never!**
6. Do not have a felony conviction for possession of an unlicensed firearm.
7. Do not have a felony conviction for possession of heroin with intent to sell.
8. Have not been fired from two employers in the past five years.
9. Don't use foul language during the phone interview

- Know how to use a computer well enough to complete an online application and upload a current resume.
- And they need to know how to spell the company name!

A corporate recruiter prepped a candidate for a field service technician's job at a $2 billion manufacturer of electronic equipment with 10,000 employees.

Following the interview, she received these comments back from the interviewer. It would seem that her advice either didn't sink in or wasn't taken very seriously. "And I told the guy to "dress professionally," she said.

The interviewer wrote back:

> - Again (he) mentioned that sometimes you have to break a safety rule to get things done.
> - Had some comments when he worked for the city, and they were celebrating workers, and he thought it was a waste of time, and they needed to work instead of celebrating.
> - Showed up unprepared... as far as proper dress. He came wearing sneakers, a ball cap and (local college) long-sleeve, dri-fit type of pullover. Not something that a professional should show up (wearing) to an interview. At least his clothes were clean. That might be how he dresses for his current tow-truck driver job, but that's not appropriate for our job... or an interview in my opinion.
> - Could likely fix the equipment but I think he would struggle with the customer service piece.

The follow up

If there is no interest on behalf of the employer, the recruiter may ask why? In that situation, I usually explain to the candidate, "The company has identified another candidate who more closely fits their requirements." Asking the client where the candidate fell short is helpful to help prioritize their requirements.

When a candidate is rejected, understandably there is frustration and sometimes even anger. However, don't let your frustration and anger get the best of you by firing off a nasty email or letter to the employer. (i.e. Why didn't you hire me? I was the best candidate for the job, and you know it! You'll regret passing on me.) Those kinds of responses benefit no one. In fact, some companies and recruiters keep those on file for future reference – in the "do not consider" folder.

If the employer is interested, the next step(s) may include a phone interview with the employer before an on-site interview. Before any direct contact between the candidate and employer, the recruiter will prep the candidate regarding the company, culture, the hiring manager, etc. The recruiter also will support the candidate through the entire process – keeping the lines of communication open and assisting with the interview process, negotiating any offer(s) and "closing the deal."

Throughout the process, the recruiter maintains regular contact with the employer as well as the candidate to monitor the process.

Selecting a Recruiter

To find a recruiter, use word of mouth, referrals, and references. These are usually the best first steps. This will suggest whether or not it is a reputable agency. Most recruiters specialize by function, industry, company or geography. It's OK to ask.

Your recruiter must demonstrate respect for you, the candidate. He will do this by returning phone calls in a timely fashion, keeping commitments and by acting in a professional and courteous manner. A good recruiter should not "slam" your resume to employers without notice.

Being a good candidate

The recruiter-candidate relationship is a two-way street. I just explained what you should expect from your recruiter. This is what your recruiter should expect from you:

1. A good candidate presents a concise, clear and honest resume that is no more then two pages. The resume should include dates of employment and should not contain any tricks of deception (i.e. when you list a college, it implies a degree)
2. A good candidate does not ask for too many details, too early in the process (i.e.
3. benefits, vacation, etc.) and is always honest about salary, interest in the job, availability, etc.
4. Good candidates inform their recruiters if they recently have been presented to the employer or recently applied directly. They do not try to get "in the backdoor" to the employer.
5. Good candidates do not work with multiple recruiters without informing them. It is important to realize if someone was sending a resume to ten firms, the little additional benefit would not be realized, since the chance of overlap is much higher.
6. Good candidates do not become a nuisance with numerous phone calls to either the
7. employer or the recruiter. I like a candidate that follows up once a week. It shows they value your service and are serious about making a move.

A final thought: If you're not getting a definite answer from the company, assume that you don't have the job and keep looking. On the other hand, if you haven't been declined, you haven't been declined. You're still in the running.

Although not hearing can be frustrating, most employers don't string candidates along. If things are dragging on, many recruiters will intervene and decline sooner rather than later. It's not in anyone's best interest to string someone along. Also, if a company is stringing you along, there's a message there: Do you really want to work at a place like that?

Chapter 4 - The Dreaded Screening Software

Mission Impossible – I counted ten different top screening software listed on the Internet. Certainly there are more serving tens of thousands employers. With many different "Applicant Tracking Systems," "Recruiting Tools," and "Talent Acquisition Software," serving employers listing a specific job opening, one approach does not fit all.

Most resumes submitted to software screening get rejected. So what to do? A review of articles on the Internet has many suggestions but there is no one perfect solution for all the variables. There is not one solution only improving the odds with some basics. As I am reading articles, everyone has a solution; they do not always agree. Below is my best advice:

- Develop two resumes. One is a handout and used as an email attachment; the other for the software to read. The second is the same information without borders, shadings, and tables (see sample). Save the second as a "save as" text document for software scanning.
- Do not place information in footers and headers. Software might not be able to read the information.
- Each basic resume is modified for the specific employer's advertised keywords. Put keywords in the Summary of Qualifications at the top of the resume and the body using bullets if possible.
- Everyone says use keywords that relate to the ad, maybe moderately. Will it get you past the dreaded software screening? Or will the excessive keywords get you thrown out by the recruiter? They usually have a minute or less for the first screening. Talk the language of the employer, but best tell your story to make you stand out. Concentrate on design, balance, readability, and your values.
- Review professionally created samples from the Internet. Note the section titles; use the most recognized such as Summary of Qualification, Professional Experience, Work Experience, Skills, Technical Skills, Training, Education, Volunteerism, Achievements, and Certifications.
- Spell out certification, titles and include the acronym such as Certified Public Accountant (CPA) in parentheses.
- Avoid the software by targeting smaller companies where you can contact the decision- makers.

- Research job descriptions, companies, and company employees using company websites, LinkedIn, Occupational Outlook Handbook of the US Department of Labor online, Dun and Bradstreet and Reference USA at the library or online with a library card.
- Be creative, applying online is the first step. Always attempt to send additional resumes with perfect formatting directly as an email attachment, mail a copy, have a network contact hand carry or stop by the company. Always bring an extra copy of your formatted resume with you to an interview

Samples: My client developed a resume for a handout and another for the software scanner. Two resumes allow you to create a well-designed resume and one that the software can follow. The alternative is to complete one resume and save it as a text format without boxes and borders. After completing the resume "save-as" a text. There is disagreement as to what font will be easy for the software to read. Verdana or Tahoma at 11 point or larger are possibilities.

Donald E. Jones

1084 Jefferson Drive
Cleveland, Ohio 44999
440.653.9999
djones@gmail.com

Summary of Qualifications

Recently earned an Associate Degree in electronic engineering in addition to a certification in electronic engineering technologies. Application oriented electronic and electrical education with strong mathematical knowledge. Also extensive customer service/sales experience, involvement in organizing work, managing work crews, and mechanical problem solver. Education is accredited by the Engineering Technology Accreditation Commission of ABET. www.abet.org

Profile

With a clear understanding that the new workplace requires constant upgrading of skills and knowledge, for me this is both challenging and rewarding. Inquisitive mind as to how electromechanical things work; maintain a high benchmark of quality service of myself and my peers; develop long term relationships with the cliental serviced. High energy; learns new skills quickly; self-motivated; timely; reliable; realizes the importance of meeting deadlines as scheduled; and capable of organizing a variety of responsibilities.

Education and Technical Skills

Associate of Applied Science
Electronic Engineering Technologies-Applied Electronics
Lorain County Community College-2015

Technical Certificate in Electronic Engineering Technologies
Lorain County Community College-2014

3.6 GPA – Dean's list three times

- Electrical Circuits I&II
- Fabrication Processes for Electronics
- Digital Electronics
- A/C Electrical Power and Devices
- Technical Problem Solving
- Technical Mathematics I&II
- PLC I
- IPC J-STD-001 Soldering Certificate

Completing ELCT 221- Microcontrollers and ELCT 223 – Electronic Devices

Cleveland Learning Center - Microsoft Office software Word, Excel, Outlook – 2013

Donald E. Jones

1084 Jefferson Drive
Cleveland, Ohio 44999
440.653.9999
djones@gmail.com

Summary of Qualifications

Recently earned an Associate Degree in electronic engineering in addition to a certification in electronic engineering technologies. Application oriented electronic and electrical education with strong mathematical knowledge. Also extensive customer service/sales experience, involvement in organizing work, managing work crews, and mechanical problem solver. Education is accredited by the Engineering Technology Accreditation Commission of ABET. www.abet.org

Profile

With a clear understanding that the new workplace requires constant upgrading of skills and knowledge, for me this is both challenging and rewarding. Inquisitive mind as to how electromechanical things work; maintain a high benchmark of quality service of myself and my peers; develop long term relationships with the cliental serviced. High energy; learns new skills quickly; self-motivated; timely; reliable; realizes the importance of meeting deadlines as scheduled; and capable of organizing a variety of responsibilities.

Education and Technical Skills

Associate of Applied Science
Electronic Engineering Technologies-Applied Electronics
Cleveland County Community College-2015

Technical Certificate in Electronic Engineering Technologies
Cleveland County Community College-2014
3.6 GPA – Dean's list three times

Electrical Circuits I&II
Fabrication Processes for Electronics
Digital Electronics
A/C Electrical Power and Devices

Technical Problem Solving
Technical Mathematics I&II
PLC I
IPC J-STD-001 Soldering Certificate

Completing ELCT 221- Microcontrollers and ELCT 223 – Electronic Devices
Cleveland Learning Center - Microsoft Office software Word, Excel, Outlook – 2013

Chapter 5 – Any Road Will Take You There

> *Would you tell me, please, which way I ought to go from here?*
>
> *That depends a good deal on where you want to get to, said the cat.*
>
> *I don't much care where, said Alice.*
>
> *Then it doesn't matter which way you go, said the Cat.*
>
> *So long as I get somewhere, Alice added as an explanation.*
>
> *Oh, you're sure to do that, said the Cat, if you Only walk long enough. –*
>
> From Alice in Wonderland

The Cheshire Cat might be the best example of where most of us have been with careers and jobs. With an ever changing, dynamic job market, finding stable employment is a difficult challenge. We live in an age where jobs include temporary, part-time, downsizing, core employees, contracted services, specialized skills, reduced benefits, and self-employment.

You need to bring some order to career choices, educational opportunities, and long-term planning. Determining the direction of the job market today and securing employment requires aggressively finding information, developing networks, continuing education and discovering passions.

Creating a resume starts with a clear understanding of who you are and what you want and need. A recruiter recently complained that she only had three candidates for an excellent technical field representative position. I said you must have dozens of applications. She said yes, "but most applicants were inappropriate for the stated requirements." She said, "Like they just applied for any job without much thought."

Earlier, I felt I would become independently wealthy by rehabilitating houses (the housing market taught me differently). I attended a seminar created by a man who buys and sells properties and made a great deal of money. I think his seminars might have made him, even more, money. His approach was a prescription for most of the life's tasks. As a career counselor, I have worked with my clients using this approach.

He said, "I do not buy a property until I know the end result." He started with the market, location, properties that have sold and were for sale, the level of the housing surrounding the property, and the possible selling price. Then he worked backward determining what repairs needed to be done, how long it would be on the market, what improvements would match the neighborhood, what would be a realistic offering price.

Knowing the end before you start improves the odds for success. Let's look at jobs and careers.
You know a lot about yourself. You know what you like and what you do not like. Some jobs would excite you; others will turn you off. Many workers perform jobs they do not like, but find the jobs provide benefits that allow for financial independence, support of the family or because of limited opportunities in a community.

The U.S. Department of Labor reports more than 10,000 job titles. If you are currently looking for employment, find a job that fits you and that you will perform with passion or maybe satisfies you.

In the 1950s, John Holland, psychologist, developed a theory that most people are one of six personality types: realistic, investigative, artistic, social, enterprising, and conventional. In is not a perfect representation of all the personality types, but it provides an opportunity to understand more about your personality as it relates to the world of work.

Wikipedia reports:
> *According to the Committee on Scientific Awards, John L. Holland's research shows that personalities seek out and flourish in career environments they fit and that jobs and career environments are classifiable by the personalities that flourish in them.*

The theory appears in many interest and personality tests, and the concepts are used extensively in career counseling even today. The best way to understand how this applies to your situation is to look at a Holland Hexagon.

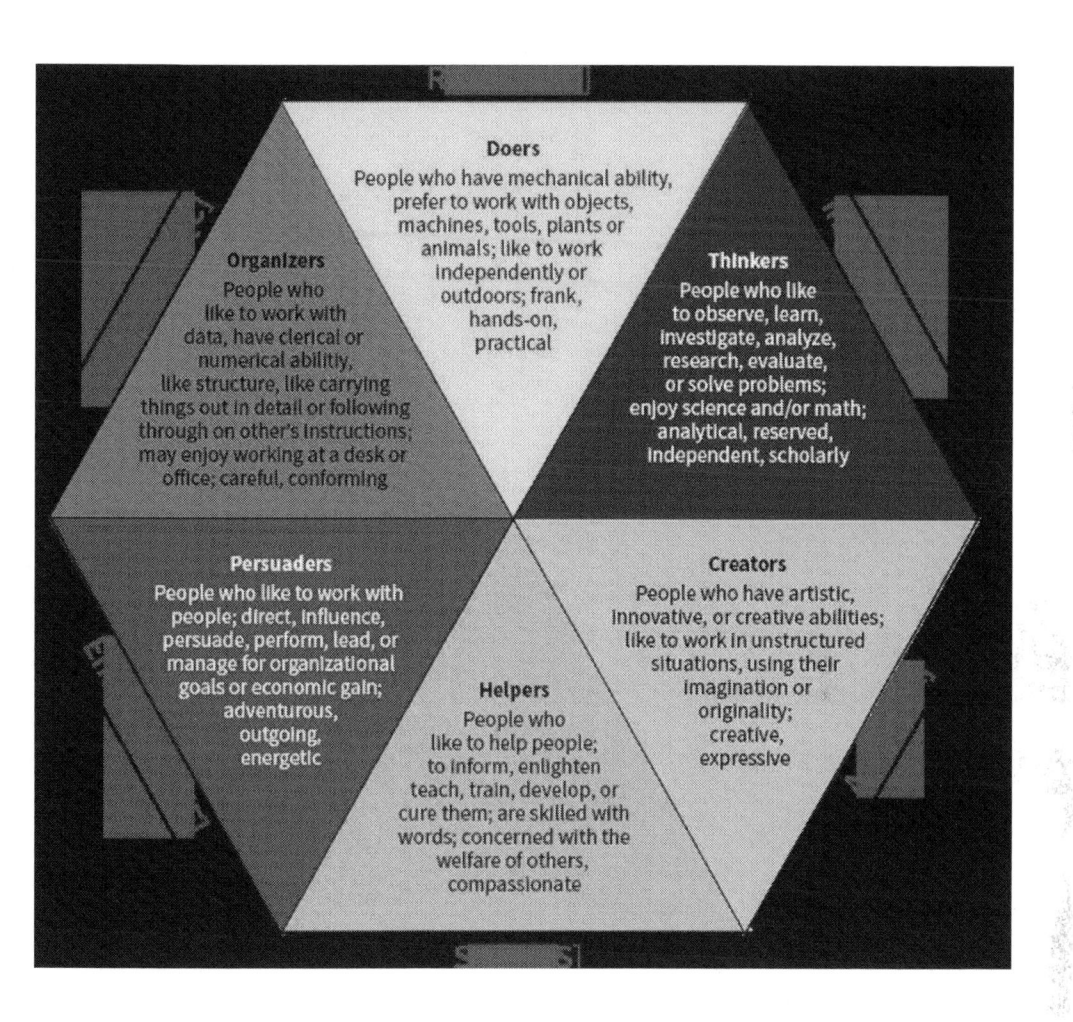

Doers
People who have mechanical ability, prefer to work with objects, machines, tools, plants or animals; like to work independently or outdoors; frank, hands-on, practical

Organizers
People who like to work with data, have clerical or numerical abilitiy, like structure, like carrying things out in detail or following through on other's instructions; may enjoy working at a desk or office; careful, conforming

Thinkers
People who like to observe, learn, investigate, analyze, research, evaluate, or solve problems; enjoy science and/or math; analytical, reserved, independent, scholarly

Persuaders
People who like to work with people; direct, influence, persuade, perform, lead, or manage for organizational goals or economic gain; adventurous, outgoing, energetic

Helpers
People who like to help people; to inform, enlighten teach, train, develop, or cure them; are skilled with words; concerned with the welfare of others, compassionate

Creators
People who have artistic, innovative, or creative abilities; like to work in unstructured situations, using their imagination or originality; creative, expressive

Image from Edison Community College in Ohio

A simplified version of the theory is that as you grow up, you find ways to address life's problems and issues. As you gain success, these patterns become part of your strengths and interests. Looking at the hexagon, you can identify what is most like you. You can generalize these tendencies to apply to work, friends, hobbies and life partners.

As you go through life, you find that you need all of these areas to be effective. There will be maybe three themes that are most like you. A social, enterprising, artistic type (SEA) might run an agency helping others where creativity is needed to move them forward. A conventional, enterprising, realistic type (CER) might operate his own accounting firm and enjoy woodworking as a hobby. People seem most satisfied when they can perform work that utilizes these themes.

Ok, how does this get me a job? Review your past educational and work history. What turns you on and what turns you off? What turns you off is the most important. You are going to make a strong effort to find employment, so avoid those jobs that you do not like. Your efforts to find "any job" will show with your cover letter, resume and, of course, your interview; if you get that far.

You need to look at your transferable skills, soft skills, education and work experience to move toward job groupings that you find desirable. So define "transferable skills:"

Defining Transferable Skills: The US Department of Labor recognizes three categories - Unskilled - 30 days or less; Semi-Skilled - 30 days to 6 months; Skilled - From 6 months to 4 years. Skills not utilized for more than five years are considered dated. If you have skills that require six months to 4 years to develop, you have an asset that might interest employers.

Soft skills are also of interest to employers. They include excellent people skills, organizing skills, training skills, selling skills and managing skills. Education that has not been utilized or upgraded for more than five years might be considered dated. Unskilled work experience counts if there is a direct application.

The sample letters in Chapter 7 and the sample resumes in Chapter 10 provide examples of individuals promoting their skills, education and experience to employers.

Two Powerful tools for finding productive job grouping in real time

A career counselor might suggest that you complete testing of interests, aptitudes, and personality to assist you in determining a direction. The US Department of Labor offers America's Career InfoNet and the Occupational Outlook Handbook online for long term planning.

To meet immediate needs, there are two other approaches. First, begin daily reading local newspapers and Internet sites such as indeed.com to find information employers do not intend to provide. Most jobs are filled through personal referrals, direct contact with employers and your networks. About 15% of job openings are posted. This means that to fill these positions employers are using advertising. With a difficult job market, many job applicants are competing for 15% of the job openings.

Advertising is costly and time-consuming. Employers would prefer not advertising to fill an opening. The message is that "this is a job I cannot fill through more direct, less expensive means." This message points to a demand for this position. If one employer is having difficulty filling the position, another employer in the same field might have difficulty finding candidates. There is a problem that you might solve with your interest and background.

If you notice a particular company running ads for some different jobs over a long period, they may be having high turnovers or experiencing growth. Either way, they are worth researching to understand their situation. This might mean applying for a job that has not yet been advertised. You might be the answer to problems they are having.

In the early days of the Internet, I was assisting veterans with disabilities with career planning. Every Sunday I would look at the local ads in the Cleveland Plain Dealer. Always, there was one page that shouted nurses, nurses, nurses. Another page shouted CDL over-the-road, semi-truck drivers. Employers were telling the world their needs.

Veterans with disabilities, who completed a bachelor's degree in nursing, were offered employment before graduating.

This is real time information that should assist you in planning a direction.

The second powerful tool for planning is the information interview. If you wish to know what is happening today in the job market, contact individuals working in a particular job. Your network or research using LinkedIn or databases in the library should provide you with contacts. Ask your personal network contact if you could use their name for an information interview. This is always a step up in setting an information interview.

Contacting smaller companies will usually allow you to talk to real people. A phone call would be great. With the gatekeepers keeping you away from those doing the work, emails might be more practical. Your message might be: *"I am considering several directions in the future, but I am not sure where I should focus my efforts. Your assistance would help me develop a realistic plan because you are working in the field. Would you be available anytime next week to spend 15 minutes on the phone with me to share your impressions of your field and your specific job trends? Please provide me your direct phone number. I have attached a copy of my resume so you might understand my skills and previous work experience. Your help is appreciated."*

Be prepared to develop questions that will help you move forward before one or more information interviews. Sending a thank you email and keeping this individual informed of your progress might provide you with leads and a future member of your personal network. They may become one of your "warm contacts" when reaching other employers. If this appears to be a roundabout way to find employment, it can be the path to finding an excellent job opportunity, a tool for the future and allow you information to craft an effect final resume.

Throughout this book, I use the term job groups. You will find the same job tasks and requirements in a wide variety of fields. Be open to looking at how your background might apply in different fields.

These efforts should help when you are "crafting" the Summary of Qualification. Your summary will reflect a laser focus on what you have to offer each employer. The first paragraph in your resume will determine whether you will get a serious look by a potential employer.

Chapter 6 - No one is "the perfect candidate."

This is the real world

> *I am the perfect job candidate; the right age with exceptional work experience and skills. I have been an outstanding student, and I have demonstrated time and again major achievement in my work. I present myself in a positive manner. I work well with others and demonstrate leadership skills.*

Who is this person? I have not a clue. After thousands of interviews, I have yet to meet him/her.

We are, well, human. We have our strengths and weaknesses; we have done things we regretted later. We all have barriers to overcome. Our awareness of these barriers allows us to address these in an approach to finding employment. This is critical in developing resumes and cover letters. Your task is always getting through the first and second screening.

We all have barriers: Barriers might include a wide range of disabilities, injuries, terminations, age, a lack of current skills/experience, career changes, employment gaps, felonies and dramatic changes in the job market.

If you have not considered an area of your background that might be a problem, you will find you are not making the cut when competing with other candidates for your ideal position. A friend asks me to look at her attorney friend's resume who was seeking a legal position. After a 20-second review, I told her she was age 60. No, she said I am 59. "Oh, you graduated from high school at 17." "Yes." The law school date at the bottom of the resume told me more than she wished to disclose. She did not notice a possible barrier.

Does this mean you will not be a great candidate for your ideal job? As a human resources manager, with too many candidates, my first task was to discover who I did not wish to see. I missed some outstanding candidates in my rush to finish my recruiting tasks and maintain my employment.

Once I was able to reduce the number of candidates to a manageable number, I discovered during interviews some highly motivated people who would fit in with my organization. They were not just pieces of paper but real people with real stories that reflected their values and work ethic. Also, they had a better resume than many other candidates. You do not send up red flags that will get you eliminated before you can talk to a human being. This does not mean lying or exaggerating with your cover letter and resume. In an interview, you might need to address employment gaps, physical limitation, or past mistakes like a felony. Since the majority of my clients have physical problems, I advised addressing this concern in 20 seconds. "I was injured; I received treatment. I am doing well and can do the job you described." Get the focus off the barrier and back to skills and achievements. You do not wish the interviewer to remember that wonderful candidate with the disability.

The super salesman: Job search is much like the experience of a super salesman. The majority of his contacts do not want his product. He knows that if he contacts 20 individuals with a great

presentation and an outstanding product he will make four sales. After ten rejections he knows

he is getting close to a sale. This is a mindset. With barriers to employment, you will encounter employers who act on prejudice. You will not be able to change their thinking. You will find other employers who are looking to hire an individual for what they can contribute to the company. The interviewer's actions represent the values of the company. Where would you rather work? After ten rejections, you are getting close.

Real people with real barriers: Below are some injured workers, with a variety of barriers they have overcome. They have encountered many rejections, but found employment. Their cover letters are in chapter 7.

Daniel

CHALLENGE: Developing job search tools for a client with multiple employment barriers.

CHARACTERISTICS: Male, 26 years old, left home at age 14 worked at McDonald's. His mother was an addict and wanted his money. He had two felonies and was on probation. He was in treatment for an addiction. He was working on his GED. He worked in landscaping and roofing, catering and, for six years at a scrap metal company. He operates Bobcats. He is certified to operate: tow motors, backhoes, front-end loaders, bucket loaders, cranes, and man lifts. He owned and rehabilitated two houses and sold one. He lives with the mother of his two children and he coaches sandlot baseball.

RESULTS: Daniel found employment with a towing company as a driver.

Donna

CHALLENGE: She is an older worker in her 60's who was dealing with a shoulder injury and the resulting employment gap.

CHARACTERISTICS: She had two similar jobs, but never had to work in a formal office and had no clothing for an office position. In her previous positions, she worked in warehouses with blue collar drivers and warehouse personnel.

RESULTS: She found employment within a month as an administrative assistant.

Michael

CHALLENGE: He was self-employed and lacked education. He was combining two careers for project management and he had an employment gap.

CHARACTERISTICS: He was a self-employed businessman in his mid-forties who lacks a formal college education: He was attempting to combine two careers in project management and to reconcile an extended employment gap.

RESULTS: He loved the excitement of a racing team and always loved cars. He landed his first new job in auto sales and was assisting a dealership affiliate with its racing team. He then became the permanent coordinator for the large racing team.

Michelle

CHALLENGE: Developing job search tools for a client with a few employment barriers.

CHARACTERISTICS: She's in her late 20's; She's been a ballerina and a model. While recovering from an injury, she needed part-time work per her doctor's physical restrictions. She may never return to ballet and her modeling most certainly will be limited. She needed new direction – working in customer service with the possibility of a technical career.

RESULTS: Her whimsical resume produced two job offers in two weeks.

Nikola

CHALLENGE: Developing job search tools for a client with a few employment barriers.

CHARACTERISTICS: A man in his early 40s with a back injury retrained and changed careers. During his employment gap he completed training in medical equipment repair. When market conditions changed for the worse, he needed to broaden his appeal. He searched for work as a general electronics technician.

RESULTS: He was able to get a series of interviews from Internet ads. With one company, he had three interviews – including a ride-a-long interview. After a month of interviews, he was one of the three candidates remaining. He was not hired.

He did find employment as a hands-on technical quality inspector. He obtained this job after I provided feedback. I talked to a recruiter who indicated his phone interview lacked energy and customer service skills for a field service technician position during a phone interview.

All of the above workers found employment. With serious barriers, they were able to work smart and find suitable employment. The next chapters illustrated their efforts.

We are in this together: Most individuals with few barriers require months of full-time job search to find suitable employment. This is the norm in our job market. Think of the job market as a pyramid. The most jobs are at the lowest level of skills. This includes fewer manufacturing jobs and more service jobs. As skills become more specialized, there are fewer opportunities and people require more time and effort to find a suitable job.

A way to build a work experience: If your barriers have stopped you from finding employment, consider temporary employment. Temp-to-perm openings allow an employer to evaluate your performance, usually over a period of 90 days; then they decide if they will make you an offer. Of course, there will be employers who will make promises if you, "work real hard" and then get rid of the temporary workers after 89 days and bring in a new group. Their regular employees know this practice.

The positive side of temporary work is to fill in a gap in employment and provide an opportunity to obtain references from the temporary service or employers. In your cover letter, you become, "a flexible worker who can enter different work settings, learn jobs quickly and become productive." If you were not that individual, a temporary service would not keep sending you to their stable employer clients.

The best opportunities are when a serious employer, requesting a temp-to-perm, wishes to interview you before you become a temp-to-perm employee.

Begin to prepare before to start looking for employment: If you are a student, your best opportunities for employment are internships. The school career center is an excellent source of referral for a positive internship. Your professors are another source of referral. *Conduct your search for an internship as you would a job search. Find the best opportunity to move from internship to employment with the employer.* If an opportunity is not available at the company, get a letter of reference and make that employer part of your network.

To recap

- **What are your barriers to employment?**
- **How do you address these barriers?**
- **How do you handle rejection?**
- **How can you build a sound work experience to overcome barriers?**

Chapter 7 - Your Story is Unique. Stand Out from the Crowd

Selling you as an asset to the company

Your cover letter is the first step in marketing yourself. If you do it right, the recruiter might read the whole letter and read your resume. Much of your effectiveness in marketing yourself is with a cover letter.

Take a look at ads in magazines. These are well crafted, costly, professional efforts to grab your attention. Now notice where your eyes are focusing first. There is usually a "hook." If the advertisement is great, you will read the whole advertisement and maybe take the next step.

Treat your cover letter as an advertisement. *Craft paragraphs, that can be your main body and provide a hook.* Always customize for the position posted for which you are responding. Usually, that means the first and last paragraph.

Most of us like to read a human interest story. A story tells us about how a person has moved through life and careers - their values, interests, work ethic, unique experiences, motivation, and determination. Recruiters are human beings; yes I said it. They hire people not just skills and experience. Your best opportunity to receive an interview might be that they can relate to you as a fellow human being.

The most powerful cover letter will use a name of your personal contact to introduce you to the employer. If the employer knows the referring contact, the letter and resume will get read and possibly given preference. The logic is, "if this person is willing to stick his neck out for this candidate, the candidate might fit in with our needs."

In 2012, a study from Universum, a Stockholm-based employer branding firm, surveyed over 400,000 students and professionals concerning the top personality traits employers are looking for in a candidate. The top three were professionalism, high-energy and confidence. Two other qualities high on the list in the study were intellectual curiosity and self-monitoring (independent worker). Do you have any of these 5 traits; can you communicate them in your cover letter?

Your cover letter is the first formal contact with an employer: If these traits appear through your personal story, the employer just might be interested in the rest of the package that includes your resume and your interview. Do some of these traits come through in the samples below?

In Chapter 6, we discussed the backgrounds and challenges of five of my clients. Below are cover letters we developed to help get employer interest. These are the content paragraphs and, of course, the "hook." I have italicized the "hook."

Sample Cover letters

Daniel

From age 14 until 26 I have always worked. If I did not have full-time work, I washed cars, did landscaping, roofing, and catering. I supported myself and now my family.

I have a curious mind with broad interests. In my six years at a scrap metal company, I operated bobcats, tow motors, front loaders, bucket loaders, cranes, man lifts and backhoes. I rehabilitated my current family house.

With all my full-time jobs, I handled cash for the companies. At the scrap yard, I was in charge of weighing metal and paying out thousands of dollars. If you are looking for a responsible, hard-working person with a strong work ethic, I would like to meet with you.

Donna

I was the center of attention in two fast-moving small companies. My responsibilities included: scheduling deliveries, maintaining inventories, tracking vending-machine activities, record keeping, training staff and troubleshooting. I loved it! To survive and thrive, I needed to be flexible and to be able to handle many different tasks.

I am well organized, with a calm and helpful manner. The keys to coordinating services are strong listening skills, persistence, and determination in seeing problems to resolution. I have a passion for achieving results and providing service. I am interested in joining a team that will utilize my skills and provide me an opportunity to continue to grow as an administrative assistant.

Michael

"Choose a job you love and you will never have to work a day in your life." – Confucius. I have found the work I love. As a project manager for a commercial painting company or a team manager for an auto racing team, I enjoy putting together people, resources, deadlines, and finances. The outcome is a quality service that pleases the client. To accomplish this requires high levels of coordination, detailed planning, creativity and the ability to get staff excited about quality services.

This is my passion. I am interested in joining a team that will utilizes my skills, experience, and creativity, and provide me an opportunity to continue to grow professionally.

Michelle

A dancer and model sound glamorous. For my ten years as a dancer, I have always worked part-time jobs. I very much enjoy pubic contact providing a service. A coffee shop is fun; working at a health center, fit well with my need to maintain peak conditioning. My creativity is expressed working in a retail environment.

If you are seeking a person to represent your organization in a high energy positive manner, I would like to meet with you.

Nikola

When I was very young, my father decided he needed to make repairs on the

family car. Soon I was handing him tools while he developed new skills. Later,
I developed my repair skills, and he was handing me tools.

I have always been interested in how things go together and how to make them work. I trained as an auto technician. Through work experience, I became a heavy equipment mechanic.

My current training as a Biomedical Engineering Technician utilizes my previous skills and allows me to move in a new direction. I will bring curiosity, energy, technical skills and passion to an *employment opportunity. Please review the enclosed resume that further illustrates my skills and work experience. Reach me at 216.965.9999. I would like to discuss a position with you.*

Chapter 10 provides their sample resumes. Hopefully, the person comes through in the resume.

Your story is unique: Developing a cover letter requires a serious review of who you are as a worker. Think of what you did that reflects your values and work style; pause, make some notes, discuss your background with people who worked with you, friends and family. You will be amazed at the story that unfolds. The above sample stories started with a discussion we had about how they came to be interested in their current job goal.

Remember the "hook." What made you pause and look at an advertisement? Was there humor? Did it reflect the values of the company? Did it point out a unique service? Work on your hook; it will get the reader to finish the cover letter.

With so many to choose from

- **Why should an employer choose you to interview?**
- **How does your "hook" draw attention?**
- **How does your story relate to your job goals?**

Chapter 8 - Everything You've Read About Resumes is True, Sort Of.

It takes more than "keywords" to get noticed

My father, a steel worker for 42 years, worked in electrical maintenance repairing cranes. He started work after high school. He apparently was good at his job. He did not save the company millions of dollars; he did not manage a group or improve efficiency with major innovations. He just repaired cranes as needed and kept them working. He did help some apprentices and toured the plant with visiting Italians since he spoke Italian as well as English.

Had the plant shut down in mid-career, I wonder how he would have found work in the current job market? What could he put on his resume? What were his major achievements?

Garrison Keillor hosted a Minnesota Public Radio show, *A Prairie Home Companion* creating the fictional Minnesota town of Lake Wobegon. What impressed me about the fictional town is that all the children were above average.

Go to the Internet and look for sample resumes at the top professional resume writing services. You will notice that all of the candidates are above average. They have accomplished wonders for their employers. They were such stars that you wonder why they left the employers.

You will find in these samples, descriptions that ended with an "ed." Examples included delivered, devised, managed, established, performed, created, improved, maintained, conducted, facilitated, achieved, designed, reduced, implemented, recruited, trained, executed, coached, increased and guided.

These are action words that can enhance a resume. They certainly improve how your resume reads. *If you recently graduated and had not changed the world, how do you get noticed? You go where others have not gone.*

Where are the jobs?

In an article in 2014, Hanna Morgan cites a *CareerXroads* survey in *US News and World Report*, shows that:

> Only 15 percent of positions were filled through job boards. Most jobs are either filled internally or through referrals. When you spend all your time and energy scoping out jobs and applying, you're hurting your chances.

In 2013, Jacquelyn Smith, a *Forbes* staff member reported:

> There were 3.6 million job openings at the end of 2012. About 80 percent of available jobs are never advertised. The average number of people who apply for any given job: 118. Twenty-percent of those applicants get an interview. Many companies use talent-management software to screen resumes, weeding out up to 50 percent of applications before anyone ever look at a resume or cover letter."

The Internet is your weakest source of leads and interviews: Your aim should be to find a job opening that has not been posted; therefore, you are competing with just yourself or maybe a few other candidates. Your resume is not competing with hundreds of other resumes for attention. Your networks and direct contacts with targeted companies are the most productive sources of leads. Answering ads on the Internet must be just part of your overall effort.

So how do you stand out? This is a people-to-people business, and people respond to good stories. Your story is told through your referral contacts, resume, cover letter, and written reference.

Below is an example of a cover letter and reference that have received employer attention. The client was a recent graduate from an electronic technician program. The first is the introduction of his cover letter, and the second is part of an outstanding letter from one of his professors. He had five letters from his professors.

Sample cover letter

Daniel recently completed an associate degree as an electronic technician:

> I grew up in a household of tradesmen. My father was a pipe-fitter, and my brother is an electrician. At a very young age, I was threading gas pipe by hand and sweating copper piping to help my father.
>
> Side by side with my uncle and father I would lie on the driveway concrete and hold the flashlight, or try and find the right-sized ratchet while they worked on one another's vehicles.
>
> Soon, I found myself fixing their cars for them. I have always been intrigued by how something works, and if it was broken, how could I fix it.

Sample reference letter about Daniel *Daniel was a student in my College Composition class during spring semester 2014 where he excelled as both a writer and a college-level thinker. He routinely submitted multiple drafts of each writing assignment for preliminary feedback before the final draft due dates, whether these preliminary drafts were required or not.*

> *He brought an inquisitive mind and a thorough approach to every writing assignment, both formal and informal. He also understood and valued the drafting process. Whereas many students need to be prodded to write more than one draft, Daniel was a self-driven composer who always anticipated the need for multiple revisions. His approaches to each writing assignment, moreover, reflected a consistent desire not only to meet but exceed the stated requirements.*
>
> *His essays and informal writings demonstrated a clear grasp of the material, a sharp command of vocabulary, and a genuine thirst for knowledge. While the reading materials for my class typically require a great deal of comprehensions, analysis, and synthesis of new ideas for most students, Daniel proved he was more than up to that task. He earned the highest A in my class, and routinely brought a thoughtful, scholarly mind to each endeavor…..*

If you were an employer with a responsible position for an electronic technician, would you wish to meet this person? He did not change the world, but he demonstrated all the qualities of an outstanding employee.

I'm just saying: My college statistics course was based on the "normal distribution curve" or the bell-shaped curve. Did you know that 66 percent of the population is considered average? Where are all these average people working? How did they get their jobs? The best workforce has employees who show up on Monday, bring needed skills, put in a good day's work, and can work as members of a team.

You need to tell your story: For most job seekers, a resume posted on the Internet will not result in employment. It is only one important part of an overall effort. The resume is important as a quick way for an employer to understand who you are and how you can make a contribution. Your story through cover letters, references, and a carefully tailored resume is critical. The fuller understanding of who you are, your values and how you will contribute, will result in employment.

Not easy but rewarding: Where are most of the jobs? What is your story? Who do you know who thinks your great?

Chapter 9 - Power of Testimonials

WOW! I want some: This amazing doctor selling fish oil with additional magic ingredients sends me a large slick pamphlet (I bit once.), promising a cure for most chronic problems people develop as they age. The pamphlet must be working because it just keeps coming year after year.

Page after page are testimonials reporting, "I feel ten years younger;" "I can do things I have not been able to do for years after taking this once-a-day pill." Again, look at the magazine ads. You will find many testimonials about the products advertised. Testimonials must be effective with the financial investment in expensive ads. Testimonials are a verification of what the company claims is true.

Recruiters reading resumes always question whether you are who you say you are; or whether you have achieved what you claim. A testimonial is verification of what you claim is true. Strong testimonials (hopefully more than one) will make a recruiter pause and consider you for the next step in the hiring process.

This is critical: In the cover letter, a referring name will get the recruiter to read the letter and resume. Testimonials will influence a close look at the content of the resume. They might assist in overcoming problems with previous employment. A poor endorsement from a previous employer might stop the hiring process. A gap in employment might be overcome with strong testimonials about character and work ethic.

Did you have a supervisor who thought highly of you and your performance? As you upgraded your skills, did you have an instructor who was impressed with your grasp of the subject matter; your passion and commitment? Have you kept up with a co-worker who had positive impressions of your work performance and character?

Most job applicants provide a list of references a recruiter could contact: The recruiter and the applicant hope that making contact with these references will not be time-consuming and involve phone tag. What if references do not return calls to the recruiter timely or not at all? Will this affect consideration of hiring applicants? Earlier, I said that finding a job is an accident, and your job is to improve the odds. Testimonials improve the odds.

But wait, you are not ready to start contacting people and asking for letters of recommendation. Requesting written references involves skill and planning. Before asking, have a basic resume available for the reference. No one but you understands your detailed work history. Their reference letter or paragraph will improve after understanding more about your skills and experience.

Ask them to review the resume and offer any suggestions. Involve them in your project (job search). Thank them in person or write a note. Keep them updated on your progress. Later, they might be a source of leads as a part of your network.

Their time is valuable: Some will write a carefully crafted letter; others might be more comfortable responding to your email with a paragraph or two. Some references asked the client to write the letter that they would sign. I had a client include a paragraph of endorsement in her cover letter that was most effective. Others have utilized a two-column resume to include the reference in the first column (see sample resumes).

Sample References: The following are sample references my clients received. This might help you understand the power of the testimonial.

> Ms. Smith has an appealing, can-do personality. She works well with others and quickly adjusted to this learning setting. An enthusiastic worker with high personal standards, she is persistent in finding quality solutions to problems. She seeks input and accepts and implements constructive guidance"- Van Smith, M. Ed. Linda B. Jones, M.Ed.

> I would like to recommend Virginia Jones for employment in the social service field. She previously worked as a primary case manager. I have known Virginia for 43 years. I have observed her accomplish many goals in her life as well as be a constant inspiration to others who have had many trials and tribulation throughout her life.

> Virginia has passion, commitment, and enthusiasm for helping others while in the social service field. In her field, she brought a commitment to advocating relentlessly for her clients needs. She has developed personal and professional skills to be able to communicate effectively across economic, social, spiritual and educational lines. Her ability for encouraging others towards self-improvement and setting attainable goals is outstanding. - Bernadette Smith, PhD

> Donna Smith worked for our family business, Ajax Trucking Co., for more than 30 years. During that time, we do not know what we

would have done without her. Donna worked directly for my brother who unfortunately passed away in 2006. When my brother was away and often when he wasn't, Donna ran the business. Whenever a problem came up she was everyone's "go to" person to solve the problem.

Donna was the glue that held the day-to-day business together. It was nice to have someone on the team with a brain and the initiative to get things done." - Martin Jones, President, Jones Coal & Coke

I am writing to recommend Michael Smith. He served as crew chief for my race team for three years, and I can honestly say we could not have operated or been successful without his enormous and tireless contribution to our efforts. Michael was always one step ahead of our problems and took great personal pride in the quality of his work and the results of our team. Michael is an honest, loyal, intelligent man whom I was extremely lucky to have on my team, and highly recommend him for your team." - Christopher Smith

Hopefully, you have references that will provide strong testimonials. Use them in a creative manner. Some applicants develop a portfolio with written testimonials and documentation on certifications and completion of studies. Others send the letters with the cover letters and resumes. Others use the two-column resume that has received positive responses from employers. Try out several approaches to see what works for you.

Chapter 10 – Your "Draft" Resume, a Work in Progress

In Chapter 1, we discussed designing a resume or the physical appearance of a resume. This chapter will focus on the content and how it presents your qualifications and personal qualities to an employer.

Will the perfect resume get you the perfect job? Probably not! Will a poor resume get you screened out? Absolutely! A less than perfect resume might help get the job if it fits nicely into the overall package of work samples.

The resume is a part of the package of your work samples. The human resource specialist is an evaluator trying to answer the questions: who is the person and how do they fit into the organization?

In my previous work in HR (personnel at the time), I start by reviewing all documentation that included cover letters, references and resumes.

I contacted the individual by phone. I evaluated how they respond to my questions and request to meet face-to-face. I had an impression at that time of their interpersonal skills through the phone contact.

When we met I noted their promptness, they carried themselves, the handshake, their overall appearance. The interview provided additional information, so did the discussion of their resume.

Why is this relevant? A skilled human resource specialist (some are not so skilled), will go through the same process. Does the resume match all other information and impressions? Are all impressions and information consistent and factual? Can I trust this person? Does he or she meet the needs of the organization?

This chapter provides a detailed discussion of resumes that will not get screened out and will provide a clear picture of who you are and how you can contribute to an organization. Most important, the resume is a work in progress that is customized to address the particular employment goals and/or jobs you are seeking.

We approach the construction of a resume as a series of problems to be resolved.

Recently, I lost my bookkeeper. I handed my new accountant a mess that included a spreadsheet, end of the year forms, reports I did not send to government agencies, etc. Two weeks later he handed me a finished product; all problems resolved. A major league batter hitting .197 has a series of problems to resolve, as does his batting coach. A customer service representative is a problem solver.

Your job search presents a series of ongoing problems to address. Your understanding of the issues and skill in addressing these will affect outcomes. The resume can address these problems or possible barriers to getting through the first sort.

Chapter 1 discussed designing a resume. A poor design will surely get you "screened out." The following illustration, an extreme example, violates good design, positive presentation of the individual, factual accuracy, and common sense.

My design of his resume below is not the perfect resume. *One size fits all*, does not exist. Later you will see sample resumes with different formats to resolve different problems. Professional resume writers on the Internet have additional sample formats that might fit your needs.

Please give me a challenge

A friend asked me to assist her 36-year old nephew redesign his resume. A friend of the family helped with his resume, and provided him a job. The resume was six pages. The last page was a list of references with their complete information. It had normal spacing and some double spacing between each paragraph. The first paragraph was identical to the cover letter indicating he was a self-motivated, energetic university graduate (of 15 years ago).

In the resume, he included all his extracurricular activities from college 15 years earlier. In the first paragraph, he identified three years of management experience that was not addressed in the body of the resume.

He worked an assortment of jobs including seven years as a baggage handler and part-time work as a bartender. And, he was terminated from his last job. He listed long lists of tasks he completed in each job.

In our interview, he presented himself as a very nice, intelligent person with good interpersonal skills and good technical skills. Was it a hopeless situation?

How many issues have you identified that needed to be addressed?

This was easy

Because of the many barriers he faced, the cover letter needed to set up a positive resume. The first paragraph was "the hook" with a little humor. The second paragraph attempted to create some order and make sense of his work history.

> *While working full time, I received exceptional customer service training as a part-time bartender for five years. This work required a balance between developing positive relations with customers, dealing with sometimes stressful situations and always problem resolution when needed. A test of my effectiveness was a large number of returning customers.*

> *Like many young students in college, I found myself moving in the wrong direction. Coursework came easy, but it was not intellectually challenging. My minor in business information technology at Kent State was of great interest, but I did not pursue it in my first job. With additional training and work experience, I found a direction that involves problem resolution with highly detailed technical programs. This is my passion.*

Hopefully, the cover letter piqued interest and led to the human resource specialist actually reading the resume. If the cover letter had a referral name, in the beginning, the resume would

get read. We will construct a resume that flows from the cover letter and presents the employer with a capable candidate.

Before starting the resume, a review of the job goals and targeted employers is required. What are the requirements of the posted position? How do my skills, training, and work experience fit with these requirements? Can I explain how my transferable skills can be utilized in a job that I have not previously performed?

How will I overcome the barriers preventing me from obtaining an interview?

The sample that follows will target work in a medical setting with the goal of eventually working as a certified medical billing specialist. Before the job search, the candidate needs to research medical settings and the grouping of jobs that are needed with his skills, training, and experience.

First and Last

Problem 1 - The most important part of the resume is the **Summary of Qualifications** at the top of the resume. *It should be created last to include all the best content from the resume that qualifies him for the position desired.* In a buyer's market, the summary indicates the skills, knowledge and training you have to solve the employer's problem. You have 10 seconds or less to convince the human resources specialist to read the entire resume.

Jack Smith	1216 Texas Ave.
 Painesville, Ohio 44999
 Cell 216-410-9999
 jsmith312@gmail.com

Summary of Qualifications

Currently completing medical billing certification program, extensive customer service at the help desk, online, phone contacts, in person, excel at technical, detailed analysis and problem resolution.

Problem 2 – Despite the series of seemly unrelated jobs after graduation, Mr. Smith developed skills and has traits that would be an asset to the right organization. The next section provides statements about his characteristics and understanding of customer service and academic success.

Profile and Achievements

I am well organized, with a calm and helpful manner. The key to service is strong listening skills, persistence and determination in seeing problems to resolution. I have extensive training and interest in data analysis and management.

I have a clear understanding that my future careers depend on constantly upgrading my knowledge that will make me valuable to any organization. My academic achievements
demonstrate my ability to acquire and utilize information.

Problem 3 – Mr. Smith's best quality is his educational achievements. It demonstrates a bright individual searching for the direction that best utilizes his abilities, personal characteristics and interests. Many resumes place education at the end or not at all. There is no right answer.

Education and Technical Skills

Brecksville Community College Current GPA:3.8/4.0 - Medical Billing Certificate, September 2014 – Current Medical Terminology, Medical Coding (CPT/ICD-10), Medical Insurance

Painesville Community College GPA: 3.7/4.0 - Computer Information Systems – Web Design Fundamentals, Visual Basic, Microsoft Access, UNIX operation

Iowa State University - Bachelors of Science Hospitality Management, minor in business IT GPA: 3.3/4.0

Problem 4 – The example of the first resume lists tasks completed for each job. The employer wants to know what skills, knowledge and abilities meet the requirements of the advertised position. Listing tasks for the employer to determine if these relate to the company's needs will surely get the resume rejected.

You developed your qualification through education and work experience. Make it easy for the employer to relate to these qualifications.

Strengths and Core Skills

Extensive customer service experience – in person, online and phone. Bookkeeping, record management, data processing	Training and experience with computer information systems that require high degree of analytical and detail information processing	Working Knowledge of web software, Visual Basic, MS Access, Word, Excel, UNIX, Xpeditor- electronic transaction software, medical terminology & coding

Problem 5 – Where do you want the employer to focus attention? Your job titles are important. They need to be common enough that the potential employer understands the kind of work you performed. Also, this might help the scanning software looking for keywords.

The company name, briefly your responsibilities and mission of the company, are important. Dates are last, particularly if you have employment gaps. Note the general dates of the part-time jobs. Including these jobs will suggest a motivated individual who developed additional skills. Community activities serve the same purpose.

Professional Experience

Technical Help Desk – International Data Corp. (IDC) - electronic transaction management and managing the revenue cycles of labs   April 2015 –Aug. 2015

Bookkeeper/Cashier – World Health Food Supermarket Managed the accounting and bookkeeping, open and closing duties, customer service   Oct. 2014 - April 2015

Customer Service Agent - Sprint Airlines, movement of baggage/mail/cargo through the warehouse/terminal area to the aircraft.   Jan. 2007 - June 2014

Assistant Manager – Panera Bread, responsible for dai operations, training   2000 - 2003

Bartender – Jackie's Tavern, John and Moe's - Part-time while employed   2002 - 2012

Please! Please! Please! Do not put at the end of the resume – "References provided upon request." Trust me on this one. It will make your resume look dated. The references can be hand carried at the interview or paragraphs incorporated in a two-column resume (see samples).

To Review

Can you identify issues that you must address with your resume? How accurate is your background as reflected in your resume?

Samples, Samples, and More Samples

The following sample resume reassembles the pieces above. Also, we covered the client resumes in chapter 6 and 7, my imperfect clients and their cover letters. Note the differences in approaching the resumes. Again, we are looking at barriers to employment and attempting to address them in developing the resumes.

Like Garrison Keillor's town of Lake Wobegon, "Where all the children were above average"; all my clients are above average. They just needed an opportunity to sit face-to-face with the hiring authority. I believe their resumes helped them secure employment.

Jack Smith

1216 Texas Ave.
Painsville, Ohio 44999
Cell 216-410-9999
jsmith312@gmail.com

Summary of Qualifications

Currently completing medical billing certification program, extensive customer service at help desk, online, phone contacts, in person, excel at technical, detailed analysis and problem resolution.

Profile and Achievements

I am well organized, with a calm and helpful manner. The key to service is strong listening skills, persistence and determination in seeing problems to resolution. I have extensive training and interest in data analysis and management.

I have a clear understanding that my future careers depend on constantly upgrading my knowledge that will make me valuable to any organization. My academic achievements demonstrate my ability to acquire and utilize information.

Education and Technical Skills

Brecksville Community College Current GPA:3.8/4.0 - Medical Billing Certificate, September 2014 – Current Medical Terminology, Medical Coding (CPT/ICD-10), Medical Insurance

Painsville Community College GPA: 3.7/4.0 - Computer Information Systems – Web Design Fundamentals, Visual Basic, Microsoft Access, UNIX operation

Iowa State University - Bachelors of Science Hospitality Management, minor business IT GPA: 3.3/4.0

Strengths and Core Skills

Extensive customer service experience, in person, online and phone. Bookkeeping, record management, data processing	Training & experience with computer information systems that require high degree of analytical and detail information processing	Working Knowledge of web software, Visual Basic, MS Access, Word, Excel, UNIX, Xpeditor- electronic transaction software, medical terminology & coding

Professional Experience

Technical Help Desk – International Data Corp. (IDC) - electronic transaction management and managing the revenue cycles of labs   April 2015 – Aug. 2015

Bookkeeper/Cashier – World Health Food Supermarket Managed the accounting and book keeping, open and closing duties, customer service   Oct. 2014 - April 2015

Customer Service Agent - Sprint Airlines, movement of baggage/mail/cargo through the warehouse/terminal area to the aircraft.   Jan. 2007 - June 2014

Assistant Manager – Panera Bread, responsible for daily operations, training   2000 - 2003

Bartender – The Tavern, John and Moe's - Part-time while employed   2002 - 2007

Daniel Smith

2616 Lorain Avenue
Cleveland, Ohio 44199
(216) 952-9999
Cell (419) 610-9999
danielsmith@gmail.com

Summary of Qualifications

Experienced processing/weighting metals, cash management, operate full range of heavy equipment, certified forklift operator, building repair/maintenance/rehabilitation.

Profile

High energy, learn new skills quickly; pride in work, timely; reliable; realize the importance of meeting deadlines as scheduled; self-motivated and capable of organizing a variety of activities.

Strengths and Skills

Extensive customer service experience, cash management, organizing work tasks, inspecting, scale measurement and serving.	Equipment operator forklifts, man lifts, cranes, backhoes, front loaders, bucket loaders and bobcats.	Remodeling including: hanging cabinets, countertops, trim, windows, doors, painting, dry walling, plumbing, electrical install

Related Work Experience

Part-time employment while working or seeking a full time job

Roofer, landscaper, car washer, catering server

Work Experience

Scrap Metal Inspector – JP Scrap Yard	7/2006 to 2/2013
Server - Riverside Restaurant	4/2002 to 6/2004
Cashier - Garfield Auto Wash	2/2002 to 2003
Cashier/Cook - McDonalds	2001 to 2002

Donna Smith

18851 Cleveland Drive
Lorain, Ohio 44199
(440) 821-9999
Smithd@gmail.com

Summary of Qualifications

Extensive experience managing and coordinating workflow in warehouse and trucking company. Outstanding customer service and office management skills.

"Donna Smith worked for our family business, Ajax Trucking Co., for more than 30 years. During that time we do not know what we would have done without her. Donna worked directly for my brother who unfortunately passed away in 2006. When my brother was away and often when he wasn't, Donna ran the business. Whenever a problem came up she was everyone's "go to" person to solve the problem.

Donna was the glue that held the day-to-day business together. It was nice to have someone on the team with a brain and the initiative to get things done." - Martin Jones President, Jones Coal & Coke

"We knew Ms. Smith over three months as an outstanding trainee and to possess many positive qualities that are valued in the workplace.

Ms. Smith has an outgoing, appealing, can-do personality. She works well with others as a natural leader but also as a team member. She has high personal standards, and her enthusiasm motivates and inspires others to achieve their best.

Ms. Smith has strong skills in MS Office" - Van Bray, M. Ed. Brian Handke, B.S. Linda B. Malik, M.Ed., Townsend Learning Center

Profile

"Go to" person for problem resolution. A versatile and enthusiastic individual, who is passionately committed to customer service. Possesses dedication and motivation to complete tasks given. Solid organization skills, works well independently or in team fashion, excellent people skills.

Ability to control details in a fast moving work facility; the last to leave when asked to meet deadlines.

Education and Technical Skills

Vocational Services – QuickBooks and Advanced Excel – 2013-2014
Townsend Learning Center – Microsoft Office – 2013

Working knowledge of QuickBooks Pro 2014,
MS Word, Excel, Outlook, Internet,
70 wpm keyboard, data entry 13,500 kph

Skills and Knowledge

Accounts receivable, accounts payable	Payroll, billing, maintain inventory, ordering products	Scheduling installation and repair of machines
Customer service, problem resolution	Dispatching, routing, scheduling trucks drivers	Coordinate and supervise warehouse personal

Work Experience

Warehouse Manager – R&B Refreshments   2009 – 2013

Administrative Secretary – Ajax Trucking Company   1972 – 2008

~ 58 ~

Michael S. Smith

25200 Hilliard Drive
Rocky River, OH 44199
(216) 299-0000
mssmith@gmail.com

Summary of Qualifications

From 2005, worked as Project Manager for auto racing teams throughout the country; including all aspects of team operations car prep, pit stops, race strategy, travel logistics, sponsor relations.

Experienced Project Manager, Manager and Owner, managed staff, training, budgets, marketing, sales, customer portfolios, and special projects. Utilizing process improvement methods to increase sales and maintain long term customer contracts.

I am writing to recommend Michael Smith. He served as crew chief for my race team for three years, and I can honestly say we could not have operated or been successful without his enormous and tireless contribution to our efforts. Michael was always one step ahead of our problems, and took great personal pride in the quality of his work and the results of our team. Michael is an honest, loyal, intelligent man whom I was extremely lucky to have on my team, and highly recommend him for your team. - Christopher Lee

As owners of the team, we thoroughly concur with this recommendation of Michael's skills sets and value to our team.
    – Charles and Sarah Lee

Profile and Achievements

Strong leadership, obsessed with customer service and meeting project goals on time within budget. Able to develop staff and maintain high levels of productivity.

- Vice President of Express Painting Corporation, tripled sales from 2000-2007.

- Experience in long term client stewardship; facility with process improvement methods.

- Travel logistics, event planning, expediting,

- Member of PDCA in executive management capacity; recognized by CISAP for safety record: "25% below industry standard."

- Deep knowledge of industry standards relating to safety and compliance including hazardous material disposal and OSHA regulations.

- Advertising, sponsor relations, resource development.

Major clients included: Cleveland Clinic Health Systems; Panzica Construction; Marous Brothers Corp.; Benesch, Friedlander, Caplan & Aronoff, LLP ; Cuyahoga Community College; Morgan-Zeisler Properties and Giambrone Construction.

This is to confirm that I personally know Mr. Michael Smith to be a man of exceptional dignity, character, and management capability. I got introduced to Michael through his late father, Mr. Irving Smith, a former business associate. I am a management consultant and in 2008, the late Irving contracted my company, KP Performance Solutions, LLC to help him develop an exit strategy from his former business, Express Painting, Inc.

I was impressed by Micheal's communication and people management skills and would highly recommend him for employment in an organization that wants to attract and retain people with the talent and ability to get the job done right and fast. - Patrick Kimera,

Professional Experience

Team Manager, GTSports Racing, (2005 - Present); worked as project specialist for GTSports and other racing teams. Project services to various race teams including all aspects of team operations including car prep, pit stops, race strategy, travel logistics, sponsor relations, sponsor development, short notice event planning, remote location event planning, public relations, track side professional driver assistant.

General Manager, Modern Concepts Painting, LLC (Apr. 2011 - Oct. 2011); Manages a budget of $1.5 million; Manages a core of 15 office, sales, applicators and field personnel; Responsible for the financial, marketing, sales and compliance activities of the firm.

President, Express Painting Corporation (Jan. 2009 - Mar., 2011); Managed a budget of $3 million; Managed 56 office, sales, marketing, estimators, applicators and field personnel.

Vice President, Express Painting Corporation (1995 - 2008); managed a diverse portfolio of 75 clients per year in 115 projects; Fielded a portfolio of up to 150 leads per year to meet and exceed sales goals; Supervised all purchasing activities with regard to painting equipment and materials

Education

Ohio State University; OSHA: 30 hour Occupational Safety and Health training course; Drug Free Work Place: Supervisor, annual training since 1997; 3M Certified Respirator Fit Test Trainer.

Volunteerism

National Hotwheels Convention (1992 – present): Assisted with all functions of charity auction fundraising event; procured and provided monetary and merchandise donations; assisted auctioneers; raised an average of over $110,000+ annually.

Ballarina/Model

Seeking limited-hours employment utilizing previous work experience

Michelle Smith
26881 Cleveland Avenue
Strongville, Ohio 44199
Cell: 216.375.9999
msmith@yahoo.com

Skills:
- Coffee Shop Barista
- Front Desk/Sales Health Center
- Retail Sales – Woman's Fashions
- Dance Instruction

Employment Experience

Dancer – Akron Ballets		2004 to present
Model – Talent Finds Group		2010 to present
Model – R&J Models		2013 to present
Reception/Sales – Fit 19		2010 to 2011
Retail Sales – Victoria Secret		2011
Sever – Starbucks		2006 to 2010
Instructor – Betty's Dance Studio		2006 to 2010

Nikola Smith

1377 Fern Tree Lane,
Elyria, OH 44199
216.965.9999
mailto: ns@live.com

Summary of Qualifications

14 years experience troubleshooting, diagnosing, repairing and maintaining mechanical, electrical and hydraulics systems. Completed two associate degrees in electrical engineering technology (2013) and applied science (1995). Completed an internship in bio-medical repair in 2013.

Profile

Completed complicated large scale projects on time, always given the hard to troubleshoot jobs, the most capable and versatile mechanic at our facility, always given the large projects, always given the jobs with a strict deadline.

High energy, learn new skills quickly; pride in work, timely; reliable; realize the Importance of meeting deadlines as scheduled; self-motivated and capable of organizing a variety of activities.

Education and Technical Skills

Associates Degree in Electronic Engineering Technology – Major Biomedical Engineering - Cuyahoga Community College - 2013
Associates Degree in Applied Science - Northwestern Technical College - 1995

- Direct Current Circuits I & II
- AC Electric Circuits
- Digital Circuits/Microprocessors I
- Surface Mount Soldering
- Industrial Electronics I
- Electronics I&II

- Signal Analysis
- Biomedical Instrumentation I & II
- Biomedical Design Project
- Network Fundamentals
- Electric Circuits
- Clinical Internship

Strengths and Core Skills
Heavy Equipment Mechanic/Biomedical Technician

- Troubleshoot and repaired electrical systems using multi meters, test lights and oscilloscopes, experienced with scan tools and diagnostic equipment used in diagnosing computer controls, switches and sensors.

- Lead man on large projects which included ordering parts and coordinating other mechanics and welders, coordinated equipment repair and maintenance with the scheduling and the needs of the customer

- Rewired pieces of equipment with no wiring diagram, repair and maintenance of equipment including cranes, loaders, excavators, trucks and other equipment, troubleshoots circuits to component level

- Repaired and troubleshot all aspects of hydraulic systems which include valve bodies, pumps, motors, controls and hoses.

- Responsible for the repair of medical equipment which included heart defibulators, patient monitors, EKGS, blood pressure monitors and other pieces of medical equipment, did calibrations and Preventative Maintenance checks on medical equipment

- Computer literate with an understanding of Microsoft Office programs

Professional experience and position titles:

Biomedical Technician Internship – Lorain Community Hospital – 2013
- *Responsible for the repair of medical equipment which included heart defibulators, patient monitors, EKGS, blood pressure monitors and other pieces of medical equipment*
- *did calibrations and Preventative Maintenance checks on medical equipment*

Heavy Equipment Mechanic- Stevens, Inc. **2005 - 2009**
- *Responsible for the repair and maintenance of equipment including cranes, loaders, excavators, trucks and other equipment*
- *Repaired and diagnosed electrical, mechanical and hydraulic systems worked independently and in groups*
- *Lead man on large projects which included ordering parts and coordinating other mechanics and welders*
- *Coordinated equipment repair and maintenance with the scheduling and the needs of the customer*

Heavy Equipment Mechanic - Ajax Erection and Crane Rental 1997 – 2005
- *Responsible for the repair and maintenance of equipment including trucks, trailers, cranes and other equipment*
- *Lead man on large projects which included ordering parts and coordinating other mechanics and weld*

Heavy Equipment Mechanic – Cleveland Bulk Transfer 1995 – 1997
- *Responsible for the repair and maintenance of trucks and trailers*

Chapter 11 – Where Has the Day Gone

Good management would advise you to develop a plan and work your plan. That is easier said than done. We human beings tend to procrastinate, work on the task we enjoy, or that can be completed quickly. We enjoy seeing the immediate results of our efforts. We avoid difficult tasks and those that require large blocks of time. We do not like tasks that take us out of our comfort zone.

If you have been looking for employment for a long time, you can reflect if any of these observations apply to you. With your "project" and "campaign" to find excellent employment opportunities, a little time management will help.

In 1973, Alan Larkein wrote a classic book called, *How to Get Control of Your Time and Your Life.* It is the basis for almost all thinking on how to manage your time. Your job search plan must include a weekly plan for job search activities. There are dozens of books on time management, but you need something you can apply immediately that will produce results.

The most powerful idea Alan Lakein applied to time management is Pareto's Principle or the 20/80 rule. This principle was named after Vilfredo Pareto an Italian economist at the University of Lausanne in 1896. He observed that 80% of the land is owned by 20% of the population. This idea over the years has been generalized to 80% of the effects come from 20% of the causes. While not perfect numbers, the concept appears valid across many areas of activity. Examples Wikipedia reports:

- 80% of a company's profits come from 20% of its customers
- 80% of a company's complaints come from 20% of its customers
- 80% of a company's profits come from 20% of the time its staff spent
- 80% of a company's sales come from 20% of its products
- 80% of a company's sales are made by 20% of its sales staff

How does this idea apply to time management? When you are planning your daily and weekly activities, look for those activities that will bring you closer to your goals. These activities might include difficult tasks. They may require large blocks of time and tasks that take you out of your comfort zone.

Here are the basics: Make a list at the end of the day or the beginning of the next day of all the tasks your wish to complete. This might include design a cover letter, contact a network friend for information, follow-up on a previous contact, check the newspapers for ads, check the Internet for ads, research a company someone has suggested you contact.

After making a list, decide which task is most important, second most important, etc. Of the ten tasks on your list, the first two will move you forward. The priorities will change every day with new lists, but if you complete three or four each day, you should see results.

What about those difficult tasks that require a large block of time but are very important, like designing a resume? Larkin suggests a Swiss cheese approach. Break down the overall task into parts that can be completed in the time available during the day. Again, you will feel a sense of accomplishment and make progress by working at most important tasks.

If you are an electronic scheduler and note taker, you will want to keep all your information in one place with a backup in the cloud, Dropbox, Goggle Drive or a flash drive. I am an old fashion guy who needs his large scheduling/address book where everything is posted. I have sworn off little notes to remind me; they end up in the washing machine.

You now have a way of managing your time. At the end of the day, you might check on how much time you devoted to your job search. Some job searchers spend about 6 hours a week, and they are disappointed with the lack of results. My clients in a government program are required to make at least 15 contacts a week. Some employment consultants have suggested 25 to 30 contacts a week. Finding a job is a full-time job.

Chapter 12 - Networking/Information Interview/Warm Contacts

Networks: There are many facets of networking. Your personality determines your best approach

My ex-manager at the Department of Veterans Affairs loves to meet new people. *He joined* and provided leadership in organizations, kept in touch with former colleagues and arranged luncheons with current friends. Me? My circle is much smaller, and I enjoy working with others, but I am not usually a joiner.

My woman friend had to find an apartment in six weeks. She was not a joiner with an extensive network. Her best friend was a joiner. She was able to use her friend's network to locate a reasonable rental unit that could be occupied quickly. She found three available units that met her needs, none of which were advertised. This is another example of the power of the network - in this case her friend's network.

You have heard and read that the key to finding a job is networking, networking and, of course, networking. What if you are more like me, or you are a loner and enjoy many hours reading and time with your hobbies.

I suggested to a recent client, as a professional employment specialist, that she contact ex-colleagues in the security field for leads. She said she did not want to tell them she was unemployed and that she was asking for help. She disliked cold calls. Asking people for a reference letter was a task she dreaded and avoided. She is currently working because she accidently met an ex-supervisor who provided a lead and said he would provide a reference.

She is not much different from many of my past clients. For two of my very effective professional colleagues at the Department of Veterans Affairs, the only thing worse than death and taxes was getting up in front of a group to make a presentation. They were loners with very interactive jobs.

So we preach that clients must look at themselves as sales persons while looking for jobs. Will you be able to find a job if sales were the last activity you would like to do?

Maybe it is time for a paradigm shift

Wikipedia reports the phrase "paradigm shift" was popularized by Thomas Kuhn, a scientist, in his book "The Structure of Scientific Revolutions," which describes a profound change in a fundamental model or perception of events.

He said even the most objective scientific minds when confronted with new ideas either rejected or distorted the new information that conflicts with their previous held views. What is your worldview of selling?

If you are like my client, dreaded asking for help and selling yourself to employers, you need a paradigm shift. What I found over the years is that most people want to help others. When their help results in a positive outcome, it makes them tingle inside. So, reach out to others so they can tingle inside.

Even human resource specialists tingle when an excellent candidate joins the company, and the feedback is positive. They made a contribution. You might wish to check out a new paradigm. The next time you have a problem that requires calling a customer service representative, start off with, "I need your help." Explain the problem and ask if they have ideas for resolving it. Thank them for their help. How did that interaction work out?

One way to get your feet wet with networking without becoming a super sales person is "targeted" volunteer work. With the social interactions in a volunteer activity, there is a structure and common purpose for meeting and developing relationships. Finding the right volunteer situation requires the same focus as finding the right job with the right employer. The larger the organization with the most volunteers the better opportunities for networking.

So let's talk about networking

A common complaint is that "I checked with my friends, relatives, and fellow workers and no one knew of any job openings." How many people do you know? If you have lived in an area for a long period, my rule of thumb is you know about as many people that attend weddings and funerals. My guess is about 200. If you are able to get 25 to 50 people helping you find employment, you will be successful.

In his book *Tipping Point*, Malcolm Gladwell sites a 1974 study called *Getting a Job* by Mark Granovetter. In a Boston suburb of Newton, professional and technical workers were in an interview about how they found their jobs.

He found 56 percent of job seekers found employment through personal connections. 18.8 percent found employment through advertisements and 20 percent through direct contacts. I have heard that most jobs are found through a network.

> Most significant, 16.7 percent of those who networked found jobs through "often" contacted people. 55 percent found jobs through their contacts seen "occasionally."
>
> Those "often" contacts knew many of the same people as the job seeker. The "occasional" contacts had a different circle of contacts and, therefore provided leads from people the job seeker did not know.
>
> **Note: "Weak ties" or acquaintances are more productive than those connections seen often.**
>
> My woman friend, in the example above, found a rental unit, not through her personal network but through a well-connected friend's network of acquaintances.

What if you are new to the area and have few contacts? You might have the Internet social networks as your primary network. You also can develop a local network with employers you researched.

What if you live in a small town or rural area with limited contacts and jobs? An employment specialist gave me sage advice. Check with the local church ministers and priests. They know many people in the area and most important they can give you the names of the decision-makers in local companies. Remember, people wish to help others, and most certainly, ministers and priests wish to help.

I was a trainer-to-trainers at Kent State University at an employment services workshop. My fellow presenter was a professor at Kent State. He said he never had a problem finding a job. He had a card file of his personal and employment network that he maintained over the years. Whenever he needed a change, he worked his list.

We now have some social networks and email lists to not only develop a list, but maintain active contact with a valuable list. Recently, I had breakfast with a young woman who was going to her 10-year high school reunion. I asked her if she has seen any of her classmates in the last few years; she said not really. Then she added, I keep up with their activities on Facebook. This is an easy transition to moving toward assistance in finding leads.

When meeting with a group of veterans to assist in a return-to-work, I had read that at age 24, on the average, a person will work at eight jobs and have four careers before retiring. With the current job market, that might be a conservative figure. The message is that your current job and career will not be the last that you network.

Information interviews and warm contacts:

In Chapter 10, we presented the power of testimonials and Chapter 8 was about developing a cover letter. The best networking result is a referral from someone who knows a decision-maker. If the decision-maker thinks highly of your referral source, you are halfway to a job.

My client, in Chapter 10, had referrals to open positions by his professors who personally knew employers. Those were warm contacts. A cover letter with a familiar name on the first line will get read as a warm contact. Since most hires are from referrals, always try to find a name before making an application.

In Chapter 6, we discussed using the information interview to find a grouping of jobs and various fields where these jobs are needed. The information interview can also be utilized to build a network and find leads. Contact a worker in the job and field you are targeting.

You are not asking them for a job. You are starting a job search and would like 20 minutes of their time to understand their experience working at the job in their field. Make sure you provided them a resume in advance, so they know more about you. Also, ask for their feedback on the resume and how it can be improved for that job.

They have a network they might share, and might know individuals in similar companies with similar jobs. You are developing a new relationship that might assist you now or later when looking for another job. Also, their information might help you during an interview with a realistic understanding of the needs of an employer.

Remember, people want to help if correctly approached. You are not asking if they know of job openings, but names of individual you might contact; most jobs are not advertised.

Building a network using databases

Free is best, but you will need your library card. Your local libraries have a great selection of databases for researching companies by type, location, financial volume, officers and number of employees. There is a learning curve, but the databases become valuable resources in your job search. Most important, you can do your research on-line.

One of the best, is the "Public Libraries' Reference USA" with many categories. Some libraries offer "Dunn and Bradstreet"and "Mergent Million Dollar." There are local business magazines and the chamber of commerce. The Internet search engines are a quick resource, and do not forget LinkedIn.

There is a learning curve with LinkedIn, so check out Internet blogs and tutorials on YouTube.

So, you have found a company with less than 50 employees and the name of the owner. What now?

If you have an email address or a LinkedIn profile, use that to ask for 15 minutes of the owner's time. Of course, you need to attach a resume or a paragraph much like a summary of qualifications from your resume. I suggest you save your resume as a PDF so that the resume can be opened and the format will stay intact. A phone call to assure that the party received the information provides a reason for contacting. Sometimes persistence does reflect positively as a future employee.

Or, I know it is old school, but it does reflect some creativity. Send the cover letter and resume by snail mail with the words "personal, do not open in the mailroom."
This might annoy some employers and cause your resume to be trashed. So what! Selling oneself is about rejection as well as positive impression. Remember the employer has a problem to solve and you are offering a product that will solve his problem. Get your armor on and get to networking.

Let's review:
- **Are you a joiner, somewhere in the middle or a loner?**
- **Can you sell yourself to an employer?**
- **Is it time for a paradigm shift?**
- **How do you build a network?**
- **Networking to acquaintances best?**
- **Can information interviews help build a network and improve your presentation?**
- **What are the best ways to research companies?**
- **Are there creative ways to reach an employer?**

Chapter 13 - Maximizing the Power of Land

Other On-line Employment Sites

Finding a job on LinkedIn:

Unlike many personal social network sites, LinkedIn is a professional network. It can help your networking for a job or not. A recruiter I interviewed indicated that she searches for candidates for higher level administrative, managerial and professional jobs on LinkedIn.

She does fill trade and technical jobs, but she does not find as many candidate profiles on LinkedIn for these openings. Like many other recruiters, she looks for candidates for hard-to-fill jobs, who are not looking for employment and are currently employed.

With her premium LinkedIn, she has access to most profiles. Will anyone find your profile recruiting you? More important will they like what they find? Like many sites where you have posted your resume, you need to be on LinkedIn but keep your expectations low. Can you improve the odds? Yes.

In setting up your profile, some of the same techniques apply that were discussed in completing a resume. Most important, keywords, familiar titles and a strong summary of qualifications are essential. A professional picture will get serious attention; no picture is an instant turnoff.

Jobs are posted on LinkedIn. If you apply, your profile will serve as your resume. A great cover letter will help you to standout. Earlier we said, read the job openings as information the employer did not mean to communicate.

If an employer is posting different jobs over time, the chances are they are having problems filling jobs, problems retaining employees or perhaps growing. This might be an opportunity to apply using some techniques discussed earlier. Remember, not all jobs are advertised.

LinkedIn as a network and research tool

More advice from the recruiter, do not blanket employers with unsolicited resumes. They get annoyed. Use the network to find people to recommend you to the decision-makers. Make warm contacts, not cold contacts.

Check out current openings for current job descriptions. Make sure you use this information to improve your resume and cover letter. You need to understand current job needs and, of course, these keep changing. This information is also useful during an interview.

Get help with your profile

LinkedIn has many features that can help. If you go to Google and ask: "How do I set up a LinkedIn profile?", there are many sites that will help. Or, I recommend a book called: "LinkedIn Guide to Making Your LinkedIn Profile" by R.S. Boone. The book was part of my education sold as an EBook.

Chapter 14 – Now What? I Have the Tools. How? Where? Why?

It's Basic:

You have probably heard of the executive who lost his job, and every morning he rises at the same time as he did for work. He dresses in a suit and tie to begin his job search whether leaving the house or not. There is certain logic to his routine. He is on the job searching for a job. To find employment, he will need to work at least 30 hours a week for perhaps 6 months to a year.

Setting up your workplace: To maximize your time, you need to have everything at your fingertips. You need a desk or table away from household traffic, distractions and noise. Hopefully, you will have a computer, printer and the Internet at your new workstation. You will need to connect to the local library for remote access to several databases to research employers. A professional looking email address (use free gmail) and phone are required.

I strongly recommend a scheduling book large enough for notes and a daily calendar. All contacts and notes go into the scheduling book; sorry no "Post-it" notes.

If you have no workspace, no computer, no printer, no Internet, too many distractions at home, move into the local library. You will be one of the regulars. All your tools are there, except your phone (unless you have a cell phone).

For your emotional well-being: A work routine is essential. You are going to work. Wake up at the same time each day and dress for the day's activities. No pajamas. Allow yourself six hours of work a day for five days a week. Plan your activities with breaks and changing tasks during the day. Find balance for your non-work time: As of recreation, family, friends and quiet time.

Your time management: Remember the 20/80 rule. What are the 20 percent of activities that will bring 80 percent of the results? You can mark tasks A1, A2, A3, B1, B2, B3 and, of course, the easy ones C1, C2, and C3. With your organized work station, you can scan the ads, modify your basic resume and cover letter and apply for jobs.

At a reasonable time, phone contact your network friends, previous employers, peers and acquaintances. The best time to make phone contacts is just before lunch and after 3:00 p.m. If you wish to avoid the receptionist screening calls, call just after working hours. Decision-makers usually stay late. Send emails to your network, then follow-up. Work on your references. Research targeted employers and make contact.

Go where others have not: Many job seekers are content to apply to jobs on-line or the newspapers and contact some friends. I recommend the following:

- Wander about. If you are in construction, visit some active sites; talk to the foreman. For retail, visit stores in your immediate area; ask to see the manager.
- Visit an industrial park for factory work. We know there are few opportunities to talk to a human being. Many employers no longer have a receptionist. You are trying to create a "quality accident" (right place, right time). You are face-to-face. They need to hire, and they will not need to advertise.
- Check the ads for employers that advertise frequently. They are growing, or they have problems. Apply for jobs, not lists that the employer would usually need to be filled. Most HR specialists have openings that have not been advertised.
- If one bank is looking for a certain position to fill, other banks may also have trouble filling that position. Employers do not like to advertise, so an ad usually means other ways to fill the position have not been productive.
- Setup some information interviews for finding out where current needs are and who is hiring.
- Research companies that need the position you are targeting. Make a direct contact by phone, email or in person. Remember, the staff at companies with less than 50 employees might talk to you.
- Visit your college or school's career center. Ask about openings but more important, get lists of employers who have previously hired graduates and contact the employers. If you can get the name of the hiring authorities, that is a bonus.

Let's check:

Do you have a workstation? Are your tools in place? Have you set up a routine? How is your time management? Are you creative with your job search? How many of your network contacts are actively involved in your job search? Are you keeping in contact with your network?

Chapter 15 - Sales Interview – Selling the Most Important Product

The Biggest Challenge We All Face in Getting Hired

By Ron Finklestein

The biggest problem is trust: Let me explain this, so it makes sense. The challenges we're dealing with today are changing. Things are changing so fast people don't know who to trust. Let me give you some facts that will blow you away.

Q: How many books are published every day?

A: About three thousand. I had my books in the Frankfurt Book Expo a few years ago, and there were 360,000 new titles in that show (and that did not include books without ISBN numbers, eBooks and reports).

Information doubles, on average, every two years. This means what you learned as a freshman in college in a technical field is now outdated by the time you're a junior in that same program.

So theoretically, if you are in college studying a technical field, and you change your major every year, you're screwed because you would never graduate. This concept explains why employers are looking for people who are continuous learners.

What is the implication of this fast pace of change? How do I know I can trust what you put on your resume? How do you rise to the top without exaggerating?

Q: If you're trying to sell yourself, what's the biggest problem you face?

A: Your future employers' don't know who to trust! That is the bottom line. Change is happening so fast today, and it will only get worse. And there are so many people marketing themselves that many employers don't know what to believe, especially during the job selection process. Because things are changing so fast, how do you overcome the major objection of trust? You need to tell them what they can expect when they hire you and why your skills are important to them.

Here is another question

Q. Who is your biggest competitor?

Yourself? That is true. Let's be more specific.

A: It's complacency!

Are you willing to do what needs to be done to make it easy for decision-makers to understand why they should hire you and feel good they are making the right and safe choice? People don't make a decision because they don't know how to make a decision. They have too many choices. They don't know who to trust because they are confused.

Your obstacle isn't your competitor—your obstacle is complacency. When people do not know who to trust (or they are confused because your message is not clear) they simply do nothing.

Jeffrey Hayzlett was the Chief Marketing Officer for Kodak. He wrote a book called "*TheMirror Test*." He states, we have 118 seconds to sell someone on why they should take the next step with us. Hayzlett says, "You have eight seconds to get my attention, and you have 110 seconds to sell to me." He uses 110 seconds because that is the time it takes to go from the first floor to the fourteenth floor in the elevator of a high-rise in New York City. He goes on to say: "if you don't sell to me in those a hundred and ten seconds, we are not going anywhere."

Can you tell someone why they should meet with you in 118 seconds? Most people ramble because they don't understand the value of short, sweet and concise communications.

Essentially your future employer is saying, stop selling to me. Just convince me why I should hire you.

The Six Questions

Below are the six questions your future employer wants answered before he hires you. When you understand these questions and communicate them to your future employer, you are effectively telling him/her why you are the right and safe choice.

Question #1: "What do you do?"

If I asked you "What you do?" What would you tell me?

If you answered, "I am a financial planner," or "I am an accountant," or "I fix computers," then you got it wrong. This is not what you do. This is how you do it.

People want to know what you do before they want to know how you do it.

For example, if you are a financial planner, here is what I would hope to hear: "I help people make the right choices about their money." Or "I help them make wise money decisions." Or, my favorite: "I build, protect and transfer wealth.

If you are a financial planner, and you are reading this, please do not use that line. I helped a financial planner develop this, and it has served him well. But you can create your own by determining what your clients experience when they work with you. Just ask, they will tell you.

I use a financial planner as an example because I sat down with a financial planner a few years ago and asked him "What do you do?" His answer was, "I'm a financial planner." And I thought, "No, that's not what you do. It's how you do it."

I told him, "We are meeting because you obviously either want my money, or you want an introduction to my client base, right? So tell me, what is it that you do that would give me a reason to give you my money or to introduce you to somebody that would benefit from your product or service (and how would I identify them)?" I got a blank look as an answer. I then asked him, "Okay, let me ask you the question in a different way.

What do your customers experience when they buy from you?" He could not answer that question either.

I would have been hard pressed to purchase anything from him. He could not give me a reason I should buy from him. He proceeded to tell me he had several hundred clients. How could he

Have several hundred clients, and not have answers to those questions? The funny thing

is that he did not want any help in getting clear. Now pretend you are in an interview or having a cup of coffee with someone, and you want them to help you identify companies that might be hiring. If you cannot tell them why a company should hire you or the type of company you can help, there is a problem.

I had a similar discussion with a person who was selling his services, and his services included various forms of alternative medicine. He was starving. He is a friend and as a result, I knew his situation quite well. When someone asked him what he did, he would talk about various forms of vibration therapy, saliva testing, and other esoteric alternative medical models.

He thought he had to show prospects how smart he was. All he was doing was making others feel stupid because they did not know what he was talking about. When people feel stupid, they shut down and will not make a decision.

In one meeting, I challenged him by asking why people engaged his services. I heard the usual, that they wanted better health (yawn). Everyone wants better health. What does that mean? He could not answer that question.

After several discussions, he became more and more frustrated with me and steadfastly held on to his belief that his clients wanted him to be smart (well trained). He was ready to quit working with me. Finally, I asked him to contact his best clients, people he liked working work with and ask them why they worked with him. He did as I asked, and he was floored by the answers he received.

At the next meeting he recapped the answers they gave him:

"You put me back in control of my health care."

"You listen."

"You took me out of that scary medical system, and all the drugs and you got to the root cause."

"I got my life back working with you."

During our meeting, we helped him craft a new commercial. The essence of his new commercial was, "Would you like to be back in control of your health care? Would you like to experience the hope that your medical problems can be solved?"

The next month, he came back with 12 new clients. He was right in the sense that his clients did want him to be smart, but he'd skipped a step. His clients wanted to know why they should care about him being smart. That was what he finally solved. Can you communicate your value to your networking partners or future employer with this kind of clarity?

Can everyone expect this kind of success? Most people experience some success. It depends on your attitude, willingness to implement what you learn, and to be open to constructive feedback. The hardest part is following the process, asking the right questions, and taking action on what is learned.

How does this apply to you?

You are a business owner. Your job as a business owner is to sell your services. When someone asks you what you do, and you answer, there are only two responses you want from them: "Wait, tell me more, would you?" or "Sorry, I cannot help." That's all. The purpose of this question is for them to give you permission to start the selling process, or eliminate them so you can spend time with more fruitful options.

Question #2: "How are you different?" or "What's in it for me?"

Let's bring this back to our financial planner. If I asked our financial planner "How are you different?" what would he say? This is really important given the large number of financial planners there are. The last figure I heard was that 89% of them leave the business in the first year. Knowing this, why would I hire you?

There are probably eight million people trying to sell me on making money on the Internet these days. Why would I hire one over the other?

There are many people wanting to help me with my marketing. Very few can tell me why I should hire them. If I ask you how you are different, I do not get a reasonable answer.

Do you make your future employer choose you every time regardless of price?

If you're a business owner, and you're looking for employees, you have resumes coming at you, and all you want to know is, "What's in it for me if I hire you?" Your job as a job searcher is to marry your skills and the outcome you provide and communicate that to your prospective employer. Don't make your employer figure that out.

If you say you are the safe and right decision for them, tell them why you are the safe and right decision. Don't make your prospect guess.

That's all your future employer wants to know.

I get probably five emails a day from people who are trying to sell something. I've started my collection of things not to do. Here's my favorite thing not to do: "We are a web design firm from China, we want you to hire us." It is ok to ask, but give me a reason! Guess where that one went – trash. Are you a job seeker sending out emails that say, "I am a (fill in the blank) and I want to work for your company"?

Here's another one: "I am a very good accountant, and you should hire me." I couldn't figure out what was in it for me. Nor could I understand how they could make that claim because they did not say. If you can't simply tell your prospects what they will get when they work with you, you have a problem because that's the only thing they want to know.

One last example, I got an email from a firm doing marketing, and it answered all the questions I had. I was ready to call them **until I read this line**: "We will triple your profits!" They didn't know what my profits were, so how could they say that? They did not offer proof that they could do that, and nothing in the email suggested they could do that. Finally, if they could drive traffic to my site, how did they know my sales process was solid enough to close more business? Maybe I had enough traffic, and I just needed to refine my sales process.

Be careful of claims you make, especially if you cannot back them up. I cannot think of a faster way to lose credibility, respect, and trust.

Question #3: "Why are you the right and safe choice?"

Once they know what you do, and you tell them what's in it for them, they're going to want to know the answer to this question: "How do I know you are the right and safe choice for me, right now?"

This question addresses a very powerful question for your prospects, which is "Can I trust you to do what you say you will do?"

Trust is a big part of the equation but not the only part. The answers to the first two questions are designed to begin the process of building trust. Your answer should be outcome driven. Tell them in very simple terms they will understand. Don't make them guess.

So what are you telling your future employer here? Your future employer wants to know how you are going to make it safe for them. They want to know how you can make it safe for them to choose you. They want to know how you will make them more effective and productive, how you make them right, how you will make them look good.

The concept here is that there are four behavior styles (Based on the *Platinum Rule* by Dr. Tony Alessandra): director, thinker, socializer and relater. Once we understand the behavior style of our target market, we can write copy, create a sales presentation, design a 30-second commercial, or create a website that resonates with the audience you are trying to reach. You want your audience to hear, understand, and take action, so let's give them a reason to do that!

Many business owners have a strong director tendency (to achieve and get things done.) If you're a business owner, and you're predominantly a thinker or a relater, you're more than likely going to have a more difficult time. Thinkers want to know it's the right action and will analyze things to the nth degree and consequently take a long time to make decisions, and the opportunities pass. Relaters have a tendency to focus so much on other people, and how it's safe and right for them, they won't make a decision until they know what everybody else wants. Again, the opportunity may be gone before a decision is made.

Now here's how this works. Many of us have one primary behavior style and then shift into a specific sub-style, depending on the circumstances and situation.

Directors have a strong need to be more effective and more productive. Here is what you need to know if you're dealing with a Director. Simply ask them what they want to achieve and tell them how you will help them achieve that goal. When they understand how you're going help them achieve their goal, how you can make them more effective and more productive, they are on board.

Now here's one thing they will do that you need to be aware of. They will test you. If you fail the test, it's over. If you pass the test, they'll likely never test you again because they'll assume you know what you're talking about. So you have to be prepared to substantiate your position.

A lot of people create a great 30-second commercial, but when the Director starts questioning them about the claims they make, they may find they cannot be substantiated. The Director thinks there is nothing behind it and you are an empty suit. They're gone; they're flat out gone. Be prepared to provide evidence of your claim to a Director.

For a Relater you want to make it safe.

For a Director you want to make them more effective and productive.

For a Thinker you want to make them right.

For a Socializer you want to make them look good.

When crafting your message, be sure to hit the points that are most important to your audience.

If you want to learn more, the book *The Platinum Rule for Small Business Mastery* can be ordered from Amazon.com or the eBook can be ordered from www.ronfinklestein.com.

Question #4: "What do you do better than anyone else in the world (in your industry)?"

You are unique. There is no one like you. The uniqueness you bring to a future employer is a great example of how to answer this question. It is not the only answer, but it is a great place to start.

Let's look at a specific example.

A gentleman stated that he was more resourceful than his competitors. What does that mean? It could mean that no matter how ridiculous, no matter how little information he gets, he will get the job done.

Let's go a little deeper.

What does that mean to me? If you're selling that to me, what does that mean to me? Tell me in terms I can understand.

"What that means is that, ultimately you help people communicate so they can make more money. You will help them tell their stories better, and you use a lot of resources to get that done. So by being extremely resourceful, you can get it done better." That I understand!

People are asking us questions about proof, proof of what works. And you have to figure that out very quickly from the questions: "What would you do for my business?" or "How are you going to help me?" Effectively you need to answer those questions for the prospect and not make them guess.

(The answers to those questions about proof are covered in question number six, which we'll get to in a moment.)

Let's go back to "What do you do better than anyone else?" This question sounds hard, but it can be very simple.

How many people have heard the latest Southwest Airlines commercial, the one where they say "Bags fly free?"

What Southwest Air does better than anybody else in the whole world is very simple. What is it?

Fun?

Yes, Southwest is fun to fly, but what do they do that no other airline does? "Bags fly free." That's all it is. They are the only airline that does not charge for bags. This isn't rocket science. If you're doing e-commerce and your competition charges shipping and you decide not to charge shipping, that's better than anybody else in the world, right? For example, Overstock.com charges just $2.50 for any order no matter how big.

If we look at Walt Disney, what do they do better than anyone else? Create memories! Amazon has One Click. GM has On-Star.

Did Amazon and Southwest raise the bar?

They raised the bar big-time. They did it better than anybody else in the world.

Think about the competitive advantage it gave them.

Are you a team player? If so, tell me how this works for you. Give me examples. Don't make me think.

Are you detail oriented? If so, tell me how this works for you. Give me examples. Don't make me think.

If I were a financial planner and did not have a high-risk tolerance, I probably would not want to attract people who have a high tolerance for risk as customers. If you are a conservative financial planner, tell your prospects you do not have a high tolerance for risk and make that a differentiator.

If people were looking for that big gain, and watching the numbers all the time, that person would not be a prospect – or a good employer. Better to figure that out early and save everyone a big headache.

The problem that I'm seeing is that everyone comes to him with a feature and benefit expecting him to know the outcome he will experience. Everybody stays at the benefits level, when what we're trying to do is move from the benefit to the outcome. Don't make him guess why I should work with him. Don't make your future employer guess why they should hire you.

Now, here's one that I thought was really good.

When GM came out of bankruptcy, they came out with a 60-day unconditional money-back guarantee on any vehicle you purchased. If you took the car back in 60 days for any reason, they would buy it back. Out of the thousands of cars that they sold, you know how many were returned? The last count I heard was 14. Now if you're selling, 10,000, 15,000, 20,000, or even 100,000 cars, and 14 are returned, that is a no-brainer. I would do that every day.

The message they are sending is that we are the safe choice, and we can prove it. I once worked with a plant manager that felt so strongly that he could help; he offered to work for the percentage of the saving he created. He sweetened it further by saying, "if I do not hit the targets we agree to I will leave the company after the first year." Are you confident enough to assume the risk for the employer if they hire you?

So, what do you do better than anybody else in the whole world? Why would my prospects care?

You told me what you do better than anyone else in the whole world. Why should your future employer care?

Question #5: "Why is that important to my prospects?"

This isn't the same question as #3, although it is similar. "What makes you the right and safe choice?" was part of the trust-building process. But this question, #5, is the beginning of the buying process. Here is where your value is created. The answers to the first three questions established trust, the answer to the fourth question differentiated you from your competitors, and now this question moves into allowing the customer to buy from you.

Will your future employers save money when they hire you? Will you create more value? If so, what kind of value? Will the organization be more productive? The message here is to tell the employer the value he will experience when he hires you!

Your employer is looking for four things from you:

Will you make them more money?

Will you give them more free time?

Will you make them more productive?

Will you create more value?

Will you save them money?

Establishing, at least, one of those things at the beginning of the interview process, helps establish why you are the right person for the job.

It's just that simple.

If your employer wants more free time, you can give it to the employer. What will they do with that time? Once you know that, that's what you'll sell them. Your employer may want to go to Hawaii, or spend time with his or her family.

With question number five, we want the prospect to understand it is about creating more value. The important thing is to define what is valuable to them.

I was once hired by the CEO of a credit union. The CEO was getting ready to retire, and he had two things on his list that he wanted to clean up before he retired. Value to this gentleman was about leaving a lasting legacy and creating a smooth transition for the next person.

Those are the only five things that your clients are interested in.

Now it is time to provide it.

Question #6: "Why buy from me?" or "Prove it."

So here's the last question. Why hire me? This is the fundamental question; this is where the proof exists. Do you have the credentials? Can you say, "I've done this for another company, and I can do the same for you"? Do you have endorsements from others who will vouch for you?

Here are some things to think about as you build your proof. In a LinkedIn discussion group – citing Doug Hall, author of *Jump Start Your Business Brain* – it was said that Mr. Hall teaches that there are five ways we can provide a real reason to believe (or what I call proof):

The weakest: Brand ("Believe it, because my name is Ron Finklestein and I built the Business Growth Experience.")

Second weakest: Testimonial ("I've seen Ron Finklestein deliver amazing results for my business through the Business Growth Experience. I have seen him do this, and he has done it for us and still I can't figure out how he does it." Not terribly strong because the prospect might think your brother-in-law wrote your testimonial.)

Semi-strong: Common Sense / Kitchen Logic (It just makes sense. This is where I like to live with the Business Growth Experience.)

Very Strong: Guarantee ("If you don't make back what you invest with me, I will write a check out of my pocket to cover the difference.")

The strongest: Demonstration! ("Here's your result. Now, pay me.")

I tried to get endorsements from everyone who is my client. That is one of the best marketing tools I have. I tell people what others have accomplished, and I know they are thinking, "If he did that for them he could do it for me!" If you only have one endorsement, use it, but when you have many, from many different companies, it is hard to ignore.

Don't expect your employer to get inside your head and figure out what it is you're going to do for them. Tell them. Right now it's about the best thinker, it's about how quick you can respond, and it's about how fast you can get results.

The rules have changed. Here are the old rules: in the past it was about seniority, tradition, and owning your means of production. The new rules are very simple: it's about ideas, results; it's how fast you work, being the best and fastest thinkers, and having the right relationships.

Many people in business today are still working under the old rules. Many of them came from corporations that have strong unions. Many of them came from Fortune 1000 companies. The old rules do not work now, especially in smaller businesses where you have to be all things: CEO, sales, marketing, customer service, operations, implementation, and delivery.

Summary

People want to do business with people who they know they can trust, who they respect, and who they understand, they can trust. Relationships are critical!

Answering the six questions will go a long way to building a strong relationship because when you talk to your prospect in words they understand, they will feel heard and understood. This is the first step in building trust.

With the Internet, how relationships are built has changed, and how relationships are defined has changed. Have you heard that some people want to develop a relationship with you on Twitter? And other people want information? Other people want a combination?

It's amazing how relationships have changed so fast and how dynamic they are. So you must understand that relationships are critical but fluid. How relationships are developed has changed so quickly! For me, face-to-face will never go away. When I buy from someone I want to shake the hand of the person across the table that has my livelihood in his hands. I want to talk to him on the phone; I want to hear the tone of his voice! I want to know that the message I'm reading on the Internet is congruent with the message I hear on the phone. Is there uncertainty in the tone of voice that isn't there on the Internet?

Lastly, if you're not following these new rules, you will have problems. That's how fast things are changing. If we know now that information doubles every two years, you must to get super-micro-focused for people to understand what you stand for and why.

You cannot be an expert in all things anymore. I'm very focused, very deep in many areas, but I tell you with a sense of conviction, I have walked away from some opportunities because they take me away from my goals.

Here is how I test an opportunity. The question I ask myself: "If I take on this project, is it going to take me closer to where I want to go?" If the answer is no, I will pass, even if it is a profitable opportunity. Another test I use is: "What is the loss that I will experience by taking on this project if the project is not in line with my business goals and objectives?" If it is not taking me closer to where I want to go, why am I doing it?

How do you answer the six questions?

Now that you know all six questions, how do you find answers to them? The easiest way is to ask people who you work with or use to work with (assuming you did not burn any bridges, so, call past coworkers and employers and ask them just two questions:

Why did you hire me? This is your uniqueness and helps answer question #4 and 5.

What outcomes did you experience when I worked for you (or worked with you)? This begins the answer to questions #1 and 2.

Question #3 deals with how you communicate your value, so the other person is likely to hear and take action. Park your ego and practice your message with a fellow job seeker, business associates, and mentor. Be open to feedback and modify your message until it is clear, concise and focused and you will help your future employer achieve the results they want to achieve.

Chapter 16 - Creative Follow-ups, Creating a Magic List

As I said earlier, employers get excited when an employee shows up on Monday on time and puts in a full day's work. And, all your job search activities are a work sample of how you will perform. This remains true for your follow-up activities.

More stories, sorry

I was working with a 21-year old injured worker looking for part-time work as an electronic engineering technician. He had just finished an associate degree and was transferring to a 4-year program as an electrical engineering technician.

He was researching companies that would hire a technician. He was contacting them by phone, fax, and email. He was able to talk to staff about employment opportunities. He had a basic resume and cover letter. What impressed me was his organization. Once he determined that an employer would seriously review his resume, he customized it, per their conversation, and sent it within 15 minutes.

Now that was a work sample! Of course, he found employment. Later he told me the employer said that once he completed his degree, he would be promoted, so young and so smart.

Your follow-up technique

When creating a cover letter, allow yourself two versions. When you do not have a name, the first version states: *"Please review the enclosed resume, which further illustrates my skills and work experience. I can be reached at 215.410.9999. I would like to discuss a position with you."*

When you have a name: *"Please review the enclosed resume, and allow me an opportunity to discuss how I might contribute to your organization's goals. I will call you on….to discuss a time suitable for us to meet. Thank you."*

Having a name and indicating when you will contact the person, is powerful when you follow through *exactly when you say you will*. This approach is more assertive and reflects your work style.

Interview

It is difficult to believe, but some applicants do not follow-up after an interview. They wait. Why would an employer want to hire the applicant? Always, always follow-up after an interview, thanking the interviewer for the opportunity and expressing interest in the position.

During the interview, ask permission to contact the employer to find out the results of the interview. And again, if you say Thursday at 3:00 p.m., then the phone on the employer's desk rings at exactly 3:00pm on Thursday.

If you are not selected, thank the employer for the opportunity. About three weeks later, contact the employer about any other opportunities in the organization. Maybe the selected candidate did not work out, and you are the solution to the problem. Also, remember that many employers have additional openings they have not advertised.

Certainly, the employer becomes a part of your network for future employment. You have developed a relationship.

Employers who have expressed interest

Whether you have found employment or not, a name and a company are *money in the bank* for future opportunities. Remember, in the new economy there will not be gold watches for 30 years with the company. Your mindset is that you are self-employed and bring skills and work ethic to the company. When things change, you will need to find new opportunities.

The Magic List

I was a trainer-of-trainers conducting a one week workshop on employment services at a local university. My co-presenter, on the facility, said he never had problems finding employment. Over the years, he maintained a list of all his contacts that could be of any help finding future employment. He knew names, addresses, family members, job titles, and organizations. He worked his network and maintained contact.

Today we have more tools using the Internet to develop and maintain our "magic list." Keeping in touch is easy. Please back up your lists, including email addresses. I sometimes do not take my own advice.

The study cited earlier indicated that employers prize the following qualities: professionalism, high-energy, confidence, intellectual curiosity and self-monitoring (independent worker). Do any of these qualities sound like you? Can you communicate these qualities?

Words of wisdom from Ed Chatlos, Vocational Counselor

Hidden or secret job market.

Essentially, individuals with a company are the first to know about upcoming vacancies. Co-worker referrals are preferred by company hiring managers because more being known about the prospective job candidate. Frequently, prospects are viewed more favorably than a completely unknown stranger. The company saves recruiting money and does not need to advertise or seek placement help both of which costs money.

The End is Near

I leave you with these last words: My friend has a high fashion retail store. She has interviewed dozens of candidates over the years. She said, "Your clothing precedes you to the interview."

What you put on the Internet stays there forever. If you would not want it published or in a newscast don't put it on social media.

I have enjoyed our discussion. I hope you will go away with maybe five ideas that will help you find the "perfect job." If you just cannot get enough, visit my website at jobsearchstrategies.net.

Chapter 17 - Survive and Thrive in a Dynamic Job Market.

Ideas for life.

If you have read the entire book and are now ready for the last word and collective wisdom, you have demonstrated the most important quality to survive and thrive – *Persistence*.

I know you have heard that "knowledge is power." What no one says is that lack of knowledge may lead to helplessness, hopelessness and a feeling of lack of control. When you know you have excellent skills and a strong work ethic, you expect someone will answer your job application. The key is current information. You are active listening and openness to exploration will help you understand what is needed.

Pause and Reflect

Because of injuries on the job, many of my clients have experienced life changes. They had to reinvent themselves. When did you find your last job? What has changed? Have you upgraded your skills while on the job or while searching for a job? Do you have a new paradigm that matches what is happening in your industry, or in your job goal?

You and I are now on a lifetime learning curve – "the rate of a person's progress in gaining experience or new skills. The latest software packages have a steep learning curve."

Over the years, you have developed a core personality that is fairly stable. What does change is the situations you find yourself confronting. We humans are amazingly adaptable. A careful understanding of the current marketplace will allow you to reinvent yourself, where others will be living in their past experiences.

This mindset will help you find your perfect job and the next and the next. You have the tools to survive and thrive.

Key Words and Concepts

The 20/80 rule. Trust – can an employer trust you? Relationships – give and get. Lifelong learning – skills and expertise. Always marketing – two people meet one is buying and one is selling, be the seller. Jobs and careers are not a sprint, but a marathon. Life is an adventure – we learn most when things do not go well, Information interview – the tool for life. Understand our culture – we feel productive when we contribute.

Second, he had value to sell a company that most candidates cannot offer, his resources. Depending on your previous jobs you might bring value to you next employer with your magic list. Your experience and resources bring value to the employer.

How do you rate?

- **Do you follow up on all contacts with your network or employer interviews?**
- **Are you timely?**
- **Do you utilize your network to share their networks?**
- **Do you bring extra value to an employer that others do not have?**
- **Are you productive quickly? Is that your selling point?**

A word of caution

Keeping in touch using social media is a great change. It can also be a great problem in your finding and maintaining employment. Employers or potential employers can see many postings. Some "fun" pictures or comments might be a disqualifier for employment. Of course, that is unfair, but it is a new reality.

Your LinkedIn profile needs to be created and updated as an additional marketing tool for employment. If you were an employer, how would you judge the profile?

Another story

My brother-in-law, a psychology major, stumbled into his first real job as a purchasing agent. He usually worked for small manufacturers and was required to find a new job about every five to six years. Some companies went out of business, others were acquired, or downsized.

With a wife and two young children, he was in a survival mode. He did not have the advantage of Internet advice or books on how to find employment, but he showed creativity. Early, he was not getting contacts from employers from ads where he submitted his resume.

He noted "keywords" for the ads and incorporated them in his resume; employers began calling him. He was out job hunting about 35 hours a week with a lot of employer visits. Usually, it took him about six months to find a new job.

Most important he had two magic lists. The first was every previous contact he made as a purchasing agent that included customers and suppliers. His suppliers had their network that they shared. He worked these lists to find a new job. As a purchasing agent in steel, he developed a list of suppliers over the years for any needs a manufacturer would require.

During the interview, he told employers of his technical knowledge and experience. Most important, he told them of his list of suppliers. The day he started he was fully productive.

How does that apply to you? First, he understood early on that work would be a series of jobs with different companies. He maintained his lists for years and worked his relationships. It is a different mindset that works at a company where there is no long term job commitment.

Made in United States
Orlando, FL
01 September 2023